CIVIL LIBERTIES

Opposing Viewpoints®

Other Books of Related Interest

CIVIL LIBERTIES
Opposing Viewpoints®

Auriana Ojeda, *Book Editor*

Bonnie Szumski, *Publisher*
Scott Barbour, *Managing Editor*
Helen Cothran, *Senior Editor*

OPPOSING
VIEWPOINTS®
SERIES

GREENHAVEN
PRESS®

THOMSON
―――――★―――――
GALE

San Diego • Detroit • New York • San Francisco • Cleveland
New Haven, Conn. • Waterville, Maine • London • Munich

THOMSON

———————✴———————™

GALE

© 2004 by Greenhaven Press. Greenhaven Press is an imprint of The Gale Group, Inc., a division of Thomson Learning, Inc.

Greenhaven® and Thomson Learning™ are trademarks used herein under license.

For more information, contact
Greenhaven Press
27500 Drake Rd.
Farmington Hills, MI 48331-3535
Or you can visit our Internet site at http://www.gale.com

LIBRARY OF CONGRESS CATALOGING-IN-PUBLICATION DATA

Civil liberties : opposing viewpoints / Auriana Ojeda, book editor.
p. cm. — (Opposing viewpoints series)
Includes bibliographical references and index.
ISBN 0-7377-1676-2 (pbk. : alk. paper) — ISBN 0-7377-1675-4 (lib. : alk. paper)
1. Civil rights—United States. 2. Freedom of speech—United States. 3. Church and state—United States. 4. Privacy, Right of—United States. 5. Terrorism—United States. I. Ojeda, Auriana, 1977– . II. Opposing viewpoints series (Unnumbered)
KF4770.C58 2004
342.7308'5—dc22   2003059647

Printed in the United States of America

"Congress shall make no law...abridging the freedom of speech, or of the press."

First Amendment to the U.S. Constitution

The basic foundation of our democracy is the First Amendment guarantee of freedom of expression. The Opposing Viewpoints Series is dedicated to the concept of this basic freedom and the idea that it is more important to practice it than to enshrine it.

Contents

Why Consider Opposing Viewpoints?

"The only way in which a human being can make some approach to knowing the whole of a subject is by hearing what can be said about it by persons of every variety of opinion and studying all modes in which it can be looked at by every character of mind. No wise man ever acquired his wisdom in any mode but this."

John Stuart Mill

In our media-intensive culture it is not difficult to find differing opinions. Thousands of newspapers and magazines and dozens of radio and television talk shows resound with differing points of view. The difficulty lies in deciding which opinion to agree with and which "experts" seem the most credible. The more inundated we become with differing opinions and claims, the more essential it is to hone critical reading and thinking skills to evaluate these ideas. Opposing Viewpoints books address this problem directly by presenting stimulating debates that can be used to enhance and teach these skills. The varied opinions contained in each book examine many different aspects of a single issue. While examining these conveniently edited opposing views, readers can develop critical thinking skills such as the ability to compare and contrast authors' credibility, facts, argumentation styles, use of persuasive techniques, and other stylistic tools. In short, the Opposing Viewpoints Series is an ideal way to attain the higher-level thinking and reading skills so essential in a culture of diverse and contradictory opinions.

In addition to providing a tool for critical thinking, Opposing Viewpoints books challenge readers to question their own strongly held opinions and assumptions. Most people form their opinions on the basis of upbringing, peer pressure, and personal, cultural, or professional bias. By reading carefully balanced opposing views, readers must directly confront new ideas as well as the opinions of those with whom they disagree. This is not to simplistically argue that

9

everyone who reads opposing views will—or should—change his or her opinion. Instead, the series enhances readers' understanding of their own views by encouraging confrontation with opposing ideas. Careful examination of others' views can lead to the readers' understanding of the logical inconsistencies in their own opinions, perspective on why they hold an opinion, and the consideration of the possibility that their opinion requires further evaluation.

Evaluating Other Opinions

To ensure that this type of examination occurs, Opposing Viewpoints books present all types of opinions. Prominent spokespeople on different sides of each issue as well as well-known professionals from many disciplines challenge the reader. An additional goal of the series is to provide a forum for other, less known, or even unpopular viewpoints. The opinion of an ordinary person who has had to make the decision to cut off life support from a terminally ill relative, for example, may be just as valuable and provide just as much insight as a medical ethicist's professional opinion. The editors have two additional purposes in including these less known views. One, the editors encourage readers to respect others' opinions—even when not enhanced by professional credibility. It is only by reading or listening to and objectively evaluating others' ideas that one can determine whether they are worthy of consideration. Two, the inclusion of such viewpoints encourages the important critical thinking skill of objectively evaluating an author's credentials and bias. This evaluation will illuminate an author's reasons for taking a particular stance on an issue and will aid in readers' evaluation of the author's ideas.

It is our hope that these books will give readers a deeper understanding of the issues debated and an appreciation of the complexity of even seemingly simple issues when good and honest people disagree. This awareness is particularly important in a democratic society such as ours in which people enter into public debate to determine the common good. Those with whom one disagrees should not be regarded as enemies but rather as people whose views deserve careful examination and may shed light on one's own.

Thomas Jefferson once said that "difference of opinion leads to inquiry, and inquiry to truth." Jefferson, a broadly educated man, argued that "if a nation expects to be ignorant and free . . . it expects what never was and never will be." As individuals and as a nation, it is imperative that we consider the opinions of others and examine them with skill and discernment. The Opposing Viewpoints Series is intended to help readers achieve this goal.

David L. Bender and Bruno Leone,
Founders

Greenhaven Press anthologies primarily consist of previously published material taken from a variety of sources, including periodicals, books, scholarly journals, newspapers, government documents, and position papers from private and public organizations. These original sources are often edited for length and to ensure their accessibility for a young adult audience. The anthology editors also change the original titles of these works in order to clearly present the main thesis of each viewpoint and to explicitly indicate the opinion presented in the viewpoint. These alterations are made in consideration of both the reading and comprehension levels of a young adult audience. Every effort is made to ensure that Greenhaven Press accurately reflects the original intent of the authors included in this anthology.

Introduction

"If the fires of freedom and civil liberties burn low in other lands they must be made brighter in our own."
Franklin D. Roosevelt, 1938

After the terrorist attacks on America on September 11, 2001, mastermind Osama bin Laden is reported to have said, "Freedom and human rights in America are doomed. The U.S. government will lead the American people—and the West in general—into an unbearable hell and a choking life." Indeed, Americans experienced a considerable loss of liberty after the terrorist attacks. With the passage of the USA PA-TRIOT Act—Uniting and Strengthening America by Providing Appropriate Tools Required to Intercept and Obstruct Terrorism Act—six weeks after the attacks, law enforcement was granted expanded powers of surveillance, including wiretapping and search-and-seizure authority. In consequence, American citizens experienced a loss of privacy. Civil libertarians hotly protest the new security measures, but national security advocates maintain that protecting the nation takes precedence over civil liberties in times of war.

The attacks revived a debate with which Americans have struggled since the country was founded, namely how to balance personal liberty and the protection of society. Leaders throughout history have suspended civil liberties during times of war using the justification that protecting the nation necessitates some curtailment of personal freedom. Unfortunately, many of these measures resulted in blights on American history. Some limits on liberty are reasonable during times of national emergency, but, as history shows, if such suspensions are left unquestioned by citizens, personal freedom and constitutional protections can evaporate in the rush to secure the nation. Examining a number of wartime decisions to limit civil liberties can help clarify the difference between suspensions thought to be reasonable and those considered harmful.

According to Supreme Court justice William H. Rehnquist, "The Civil War was the first time that the U.S. government mobilized for a major war effort, and a major war effort necessarily results in the curtailment of some civil liberties." During the war, President Abraham Lincoln constantly had to balance the conflicting interests of military security and personal liberty. At the heart of that conflict was the writ of habeas corpus, which requires authorities to show a court sufficient cause as to why someone is being detained. Lincoln's suspension meant that individuals could be arrested and held without formal charges being lodged against them. Throughout the war, Lincoln suspended habeas corpus eight times. The suspension applied to Confederate spies or those who aided the Rebel cause, interfered with military enlistments, resisted the draft, or were "guilty of any disloyal practice." The military could also arrest newspaper editors and speakers critical of the war effort. In addition, Lincoln ordered that people who were arrested under his proclamation be subject to martial law, meaning that they could be tried and punished in military courts.

Many people protested Lincoln's decision, particularly Chief Justice Roger B. Taney. When in 1861 John Merryman, a Maryland legislator, was arrested and held at Fort McHenry in Baltimore for soliciting soldiers for the Confederate army, Taney immediately issued a writ of habeas corpus, commanding the military to bring Merryman before his court. The military refused to follow the writ, citing Lincoln's suspension of habeas corpus. In *Ex-parte Merryman*, Taney opined that Lincoln's action was unconstitutional because the writ of habeas corpus could not be suspended without an act of Congress. Taney and his supporters also argued that Lincoln's intention was to silence political dissent. Lincoln and the military ignored Taney's ruling, and Merryman stayed in jail. The Supreme Court officially restored the writ of habeas corpus after the war ended.

Though much controversy surrounds the issue, many scholars, particularly Supreme Court justice Sandra Day O'Connor, contend that the main purpose of Lincoln's order was to apprehend draft dodgers, prisoners of war, spies, and people giving assistance to the enemy. Indeed, of the thirty-eight thousand people arrested under Lincoln's proclamation, only a handful were detained for voicing political dissent. Most were arrested for evading the draft, defrauding the government, or smuggling goods to the Confederacy. Thus, according to O'Connor, the suspension was enacted out of military necessity. As stated by O'Connor, "[Lincoln] understood that a democracy only grows stronger by allowing people to voice their opposition to the government, even in the midst of war."

In contrast, President Woodrow Wilson forcefully silenced dissenters during World War I. He warned that disloyalty "must be crushed out of existence." In 1917 Congress passed the Espionage Act, which permitted fines of up to ten thousand dollars and prison sentences of up to twenty years for antiwar activities. The Sedition Act of 1918 was even more draconian, imposing serious penalties on anyone convicted of using "disloyal, profane, scurrilous, or abusive language" about the Constitution, the government, the military, or the flag. Under the Espionage and Sedition Acts, both of which were later upheld by the Supreme Court, federal authorities prosecuted more than two thousand people for their opposition to the war and the draft, and most judges were quick to mete out the recommended punishments. The result was the suppression of virtually all criticism of the war.

The repression of dissident views continued after the war was over under Wilson's attorney general A. Mitchell Palmer and his assistant J. Edgar Hoover. Palmer and Hoover began to target people they believed were Communists and Socialists in a campaign referred to as the Red Scare. Their most notorious operation, the Palmer Raids, lasted from 1918 to 1921. Without warrants, Palmer's men smashed union offices and the headquarters of Communist and Socialist organizations, arresting over ten thousand people. In December 1919 Palmer's agents gathered 249 of the arrestees and placed them on a ship bound for the Soviet Union. In January 1920 Palmer's agents arrested another six thousand people. Palmer justified his actions by stating that communism was "eating its way into the home of the American workman"; he believed that American Communists were responsible for most of the country's social problems.

During and immediately following the Red Scare, Americans became increasingly critical of the government's disregard for civil liberties. Officials responded accordingly, and from 1920 to 1923 the federal government released from prison every person who had been convicted under the Espionage and Sedition Acts. A decade later, President Franklin D. Roosevelt granted all of them amnesty, restoring their full political and civil rights. In addition, over the next fifty years, the Supreme Court overruled every one of its World War I decisions, holding in effect that the people who had been imprisoned or deported for dissent had been punished for speech that was protected by the First Amendment.

According to most commentators, the Espionage and Sedition Acts and Palmer's campaigns were clearly designed to silence political opposition, violating the constitutional right to freedom of speech. In contrast, Lincoln suspended habeas corpus, in O'Connor's opinion, out of military necessity. These examples reflect the difference between reasonable curtailment of civil liberties and harmful suspension of constitutional protections.

According to critics of the USA PATRIOT Act, the current struggle between defending the nation from terrorist acts and maintaining liberty challenges Americans to remember the principles that the nation represents: freedom and democracy. These principles were abandoned during World War I and other times during the nation's history. But if these freedoms are forgotten in times of national crisis, many analysts contend, America loses precisely what it is working to defend. As stated by law professor Geoffrey R. Stone, "To strike the right balance in our time, our nation needs citizens who have the wisdom to know excess when they see it and the courage to stand for liberty when it is imperiled."

Civil Liberties: Opposing Viewpoints examines these issues and others in the following chapters: Should Limits Be Placed on Freedom of Expression? Should Church and State Be Separate? Does Technology Threaten Privacy? How Has the War on Terrorism Affected Civil Liberties? As the viewpoints contained in the chapters reveal, protecting civil liberties requires a balancing act between the rights of the individual and the protection of society.

CHAPTER 1

Should Limits Be Placed on Freedom of Expression?

Chapter Preface

In 1981 a fourteen-year-old boy was found by his mother and his best friend hanging by a belt in his closet. At his feet lay a copy of *Hustler* magazine open to an article entitled "Orgasm of Death," which described autoerotic asphyxiation. A form of masturbation, autoerotic asphyxiation involves restricting air supply at the moment of orgasm to allegedly experience more intense pleasure. The boy's mother and his friend sued the magazine in *Herceg v. Hustler Magazine, Inc.* for causing fatal injury to a child, thus violating Texas law. Although federal jurors decided for the plaintiff, the case was overturned in 1987 by the Fifth U.S. Circuit Court of Appeals, which argued that the article fell within the magazine's right to freedom of speech. This case represents the enormous controversy over whether pornography and other forms of speech often considered harmful deserve constitutional protection.

According to the Community Defense Council (CDC), an anti-pornography organization, three categories of speech are not protected by the First Amendment: libel, fighting words (speech intended to inflict injury or disturb the peace), and obscenity. In 1973, in *Miller v. California*, the Supreme Court outlined a three-part test that almost every state uses to identify obscenity. For an expression to be obscene, the Court decided that the average person of the affected community must find that the expression appeals directly to prurient interests, the expression must be patently offensive, and the expression must lack redeeming value. Anti-pornography crusaders contend that pornographic material, such as the *Hustler* article, passes the *Miller* test for obscenity, and thus does not deserve constitutional protection under the First Amendment.

In the dissenting opinion in *Herceg*, Justice Edith H. Jones argued that *Hustler* magazine should have been held responsible for the boy's death. She criticized the fact that First Amendment jurisprudence serves to protect individuals from "defamation, obscenity, and the threat of mob violence," but, in this case, it failed to protect individuals from bodily harm and death caused by speech. Jones and others contend that because pornography does not contribute to any productive exchange of ideas, it should not be afforded full First Amendment protection. As stated by the CDC, "Incredibly, the majority [in *Herceg*] decided that a pornographic magazine's article which explains in great detail how to masturbate while cutting off oxygen to the brain, and which led to the death of a teenager, was entitled to just as much protection under the First Amendment as pure political speech."

Others argue that pornography must be accorded full First Amendment protection to ensure that all forms of expression remain free. Nadine Strossen, president of the American Civil Liberties Union (ACLU), contends that any restriction on expression jeopardizes existing free speech protections. For example, she argues, if pornography is censored, "the government could outlaw flag burning and the teaching of Marxist doctrine because they might lead to the erosion of patriotism and our capitalist system . . . [and] advertising for alcohol, tobacco, and innumerable other products could be prohibited because it might cause adverse health effects." Thus, according to Strossen, censoring pornography because of its potential for harm could lead to the censoring of all forms of expression that carry risks.

The debate over whether pornography should receive First Amendment protection reflects the controversial nature of expression in a free society. According to free expression advocates, limiting speech to popular ideas risks silencing controversial, but possibly beneficial, voices. Justice Alvin Rubin, writing the majority opinion in *Herceg*, stated, "The constitutional protection accorded to the freedom of speech and of the press is not based on the naïve belief that speech can do no harm, but on the confidence that the benefits society reaps from the free flow and exchange of ideas outweigh the costs society endures by receiving reprehensible or dangerous ideas."

The debate over pornography and free speech has been a long-standing one. Indeed, issues regarding free expression evoke powerful emotions in a nation that calls itself "the land of the free." Authors in the following chapter debate how much to limit freedom of expression to protect society without destroying the freedom that Americans hold so dear.

"When freedom of expression is stretched to protect . . . advertising, gossip, racial slurs, obscenity, and pornography with a blind eye and an even hand, the whole concept loses its credibility."

Limits Should Be Placed on Freedom of Expression

Francis Canavan

According to Francis Canavan in the following viewpoint, the First Amendment does not guarantee absolute freedom of expression. He maintains that the First Amendment only applies to freedom of speech and freedom of the press, not to all expression. Modern liberals, he argues, contend that free expression is valuable in itself, regardless of what is expressed. However, in Canavan's opinion, free expression is only valuable when it contributes to the good of society. Thus, free speech and free press are the means to a social good, not a good in themselves, and can be restricted to serve that good, Canavan contends. Canavan is the author of several books on political theory, including *The Ethical Dimension of Political Life* and *Freedom of Expression: Purpose as Limit.*

As you read, consider the following questions:
1. Whose power to censure does the First Amendment apply to, according to Canavan?
2. In the author's opinion, why did historic figures, such as John Milton and John Stuart Mill, advocate freedom of speech and press?
3. As stated by Canavan, what is society's greatest need today?

Francis Canavan, "Speech That Matters," *Society*, vol. 36, September 1999, p. 11.

E veryone knows that the First Amendment to the Constitution of the United States guarantees the freedom of speech and press. Many people, however, intellectuals not the least among them, do not know what the First Amendment actually says. They are convinced nonetheless that it means something that it does not in fact say and cannot mean. As Will Rogers used to say, the trouble with this country is that too many people know too many things that just ain't so.

Limitations on Government

For example, it is widely and unthinkingly believed that the First Amendment prohibits all constraint on speech or publication imposed by anyone. In fact, however, the Amendment speaks only of the U.S. Congress: "Congress (emphasis added) shall make no law . . . abridging the freedom of speech, or of the press." Through its interpretation of the Fourteenth Amendment, the U.S. Supreme Court has extended this limitation of Congress's power to all levels of government in the United States—but only to governments. The First Amendment limits what governments may do, not what private institutions or individuals may do in regard to speech or publication. As the Court remarked in *Hudgens v. NLRB*, . . . in 1976,

> It is a commonplace that the constitutional guarantee of free speech is a guarantee only against abridgment by government, federal, or state.

Well informed people are aware that the Amendment applies only to governments, but some of them argue that governments, at least, are barred from imposing any limitation on anything that can be called "expression." These First Amendment absolutists, as we may call them, collapse "the freedom of speech, or of the press" into "freedom of expression." They then assume that anything that comes out of a human mouth, a printing press, or a motion picture projector, or is done in a theatrical performance, is "expression." As such, they allege, it is immune from interference by government. . . .

Expression vs. Conduct

Freedom of speech and press is too complex a notion to be condensed into absolute freedom of expression. Yet absolutists continually try to turn the First Amendment into a guarantee of freedom of expression without limit or qualification. In their view, it does not matter what is expressed, or how it is expressed, so long as it is "expressed" and not "done." According to them, no legislature and no court may consider the substantive content of an utterance or publication because to do so would engage government in "censorship." The content of expression is thus absorbed into its form: from a constitutional point of view, the content is irrelevant and all that matters is that it has the form of expression rather than the form of conduct.

But to take this position is to detach expression from any ends which it may be supposed to serve and to make it an end in itself. We give constitutional protection to speech and publication, the argument runs, not for any good we hope to achieve through them, but simply for the sake of expression, which is considered as a good in and of itself. The right to expression is absolute because expression is the end and is not a means to any higher end which might limit it.

Censure and Censorship

The fact that a wide variety of ideas can be expressed in our society does not mean they are all equally valid. Too many people believe that supporting freedom of expression means accepting, without judgment, all forms and content of free expression. As author Garry Wills has pointed out, "The whole idea of free speech is not to make certain ideas exempt from criticism but to expose them to it." There is a difference between censure and censorship. We have every right, perhaps even the obligation, to censure ideas we do not approve of. While someone may have the right to express a disturbing idea, he does not have the right to hide behind the First Amendment to avoid the heat of opposition. Limits in any society are the result of continuing dialog concerning what is and is not acceptable.

William H. Hogeboom, *Billboard*, March 27, 1993.

This point is crucial because ends both justify and limit means. That the end justifies the means is a classically immoral principle if it is understood to mean that a good end justifies any means, however evil in itself. But there is a perfectly legitimate sense in which only an end can justify a means. If you ask someone why he is using a certain instrument or following a certain course of action, he explains and justifies what he is doing by telling you what he is trying to accomplish, why it is a good thing to accomplish, and how this instrument or policy is designed to achieve that end. In this sense the end justifies the means and nothing but the end can justify it insofar as it is a means.

The relationship of end and means bears directly on the question why we Americans, or any other sane and civilized people, should want a national policy of freedom of speech and press. Absolutists badly assert that we treasure expression as an end in itself and tell us that is The American Way. We guarantee everyone's right to express whatever he feels like expressing, without regard to the content, manner, or medium of expression, and without regard to the public health, safety, welfare, or morals, simply and solely because it is expression and expression deserves protection for its own sake. Expression is the end and the end is pursued without limit.

Now it may be well that no one ever goes quite that far in advocating absolute freedom of expression, although it must be admitted that the rhetoric which some advocates use goes far in that direction. Still, if pressed, most absolutists will qualify their demand to some extent. But the moment qualifications are admitted, we have to cease to regard expression as an absolute end and have begun to look on it in relation to ends and consequences beyond itself.

The Value of Expression

There are evils which we are not prepared to tolerate merely because preventing them would involve some limitation of expression. There are social goods to which certain forms of expression seem to have no relation at all and it is not clear why those forms of expression deserve protection. At this point we must ask ourselves what value we attach to expression as such. Granted, we do place some value on the right to speak freely; the question is how much? Do we see this right as a primary end, to which all else is subordinate, or do we consider freedom of expression as valuable principally for the service it renders to ends beyond itself?

If we answer yes to the latter question, that is, if we view freedom of speech and press principally as a means to higher and further ends, then we shall find it difficult to justify an unlimited freedom of expression. For ends not only justify but limit means. No one who rationally pursues an end chooses and keeps on using means which turn out not to achieve it, or to be irrelevant to it, or positively to impede its accomplishment. The end governs the choice and use of means and limits the means to those which really promote the end.

So, at least, have the major historical advocates of freedom of speech and press always understood it. John Milton, Benedict de Spinoza, John Stuart Mill, and such lesser but significant luminaries as Tunis Wortman, Walter Bagehot, Harold Laski, Zechariah Chafee, Jr., and Alexander Meiklejohn, have all argued for a broad freedom of speech and press. But the argument was that freedom to speak and publish liberated human reason to pursue truth, that the truth would reveal to men what was good for them, and that the good would make them happy. The true and the good were the end, reason was the means for achieving it, and freedom of speech and press was the necessary condition for reason to do its work.

Pursuing Truth

These men were all, in varying degrees, optimistic rationalists. Their faith in the power of reason may have been exaggerated, but it was the rock on which they built their case for freedom of expression. They did not build it on the value of expression simply as expression, and certainly not on a skeptical doubt about the ability of the human mind to know truth.

They did not think that the truth was immediately and without effort known to all. On the contrary, truth had to be laboriously pursued and the pursuit was more likely to be successful if it engaged many minds in controversy and debate. Milton stated this conviction in famous and oft-quoted lines in his *Areopagitica:*

> Though all the winds of doctrine were let loose to play upon the earth, so Truth be in the field, we do injuriously by licensing and prohibiting to misdoubt her strength. Let her and Falsehood grapple: who ever knew Truth put to the worse, in a free and open encounter.

Truth is great and will prevail, but not at once. The "golden rule," Milton assures us, is "to be still searching for what we know not, by what we know, still closing up truth to truth as we find it."

In *Tractatus Politicus* Benedict de Spinoza advocated in similar terms for men's freedom to speak their minds on questions of public importance:

> Human wits are too blunt to get to the heart of all problems immediately; but they are sharpened by the give and take of discussion and debate, and by exploring every possible course men eventually discover the measures which all approve and which no one would have thought of before discussion.

Lacking Absolute Certainty

John Stuart Mill is often thought of as basing his pleas for unrestrained freedom of discussion on skepticism because the premise of his argument was that we can never have "absolute certainty" and therefore never can be sure but that the opinion we suppress may be true. In fact, however, the conclusion he reached was not that truth was unknowable. Rather, it was that we would achieve a growing consensus on true opinions if we renounced all pretensions to infallibility and left the public forum open to all views, however immoral we might consider them to be (see *On Liberty*). Truth, though never known infallibly, was still great and would prevail. In *On Liberty* Mill writes:

> As mankind improves, the number of doctrines which are no longer disputed or doubted will be constantly on the increase; and the well-being of mankind may almost be measured by the number and gravity of the truths which have reached the point of being uncontested. . . .

In his book *Political Freedom: The Constitutional Powers of the People* Meiklejohn held that the First Amendment provides an absolute guarantee of freedom only to political speech, i.e., to "speech which bears, directly or indirectly, upon issues with which voters have to deal—only, therefore, to the consideration of matters of public interest." In this forum he said, "Free men need truth as they need nothing else. In the last resort it is only the search for and dissemination of truth that can keep our country safe." Other kinds of speech can be and often have been limited by law; after mentioning some of them, he said, "this listing of legitimate legislative abridgments of speech could be continued indefinitely. Their number is legion." He acknowledged, "a private need to speak" which was entitled to "impartial consideration," but it was "liable to such abridgments as the general welfare may require."

Meiklejohn put his finger on the root defect of contemporary liberal thought (and, to some extent, of our constitutional jurisprudence besides) on the freedom of speech and press. It is the refusal to make distinctions among kinds and levels of speech and publication. Liberalism treats all manners of expressing oneself, from the most obscene to the most civilized, as identical, and it pretends that all media of expression—the spoken word, the printed word, the motion picture, and the live performance on stage—should be exactly the same in the eyes of the law.

Rejecting Reason

Even more radically, liberals today are constantly tempted to deny that there is any principle which reason can discern in the light of which we can make distinctions among the degrees of protection to which several kinds, manners and media of expression are entitled. The classical liberal argument for the freedom of speech and the press was founded on faith in reason. Today's liberal argument rejects the appeal to reason for fear lest, if it were admitted that reason can bring us to truth, then truth may become the ground for imposing restrictions on freedom. Better, it is thought, to defend an absolute and unqualified freedom of expression (or, if qualified, only by the need to stop short of direct incitement to crime) on the ground that truth is unattainable, that reason is no more than an instrument for finding the means to the satisfaction of desire, and that all expressions, no matter what they express or how they express it, are equal in the only essential respect, that of being expressions rather than actions.

In this radically subjective and skeptical view there is no distinction between speech that matters and speech that does not. No distinction is possible because there are no publicly acknowledged ends which the constitutionally guaranteed freedom of expression is supposed to serve. Since there are no ends to be achieved, there can be no limits on expression as a means to those ends.

But if this is so, there is also no answer to the question why we as a people should guarantee freedom of speech and press. If it serves no ends, why should we judge it so important that we write protection for it into our Constitution? Any answer would have to be stated in terms of the ends we hope to achieve, and contemporary liberals are left with no answer but this: we guarantee freedom of expression for its own sake. Expression is the end; reason, truth, and the public good have nothing to do with it.

But this is no answer, if one wishes to convince a whole people with it. Writers, artists, academicians, and intellectuals generally may value, or may think they value, freedom of expression above all other human goods. For their own reasons, so may journalists, gossip-mongers, and pornographers. Most people, however, do not rank an unqualified freedom of expression so highly as to sacrifice anything they consider truly important to it. When freedom of expression is stretched to protect not only religious preaching, political debate, scientific publication, and art, but also advertising, gossip, racial slurs, obscenity, and pornography with a blind eye and an even hand, the whole concept loses its credibility. Detached from the high and noble ends originally proposed for it, freedom of speech and press cannot be taken seriously.

The Public Good

Two positions remain to which First Amendment absolutists may fall back to answer to this criticism. One is that all expressions contribute in some way to the pursuit of truth and the public good. Bad ideas can be recognized as bad, but they still perform a useful function by calling forth good ideas in reply, and the public emerges wiser and better informed from the debate. That was the classical liberal argument. The contemporary liberal gloss on it, however, is that anything that can be uttered, printed, or presented on stage or screen is an idea and therefore a contribution to the rational goals of freedom. In light of what we can see, hear, and read today, this contention is simply unbelievable, and is in fact a return to the claim that expression is an end in itself.

The other fallback position (which was John Stuart Mill's

ultimate line of defense) is that the harm done by allowing any restriction on expression always outweighs the good accomplished by it. Defenders of this position will admit that much of what is published in the several media today is trash not worth protecting, or is a corrupting influence that should be suppressed if it were possible to do so without suppressing valuable publications in the process. Unfortunately, however, they say, it is not possible: a government that can punish obscenity will end by banning Shakespeare and the Bible because they contain naughty words.

But this argument loses its persuasive power after a certain point. It is true that we must tolerate much that is foolish, offensive, and noxious lest in the effort to get rid of it, we should deprive ourselves of expressions which contribute to the purposes for which we have established freedom of speech and press. It does not follow that society must tolerate all expressions, however mindless or pernicious they may be, merely because First Amendment absolutists assure us that society is incapable of making rational distinctions among expressions.

There is, in fact, no reason to believe that such is the case. We know that arts and letters do not flourish under totalitarian tyrannies, but history provides no evidence to show that they flourish best under regimes of unlimited freedom of expression. The history of our own country, in particular during the permissive atmosphere of the past two decades, offers no ground for believing that the level of thought, discussion, literature, art, and even entertainment rises as the cultural and legal restraints on publication go down. The claim that freedom to think, speak, write, and present depends on the absence of all restraints is mere dogmatism.

Endangering Freedom

As Walter Lippmann explained more than thirty years ago in his book *Essays in the Public Philosophy*, this dogmatism endangers the very freedom it purports to defend:

> Divorced from its original purpose and justification, as a process of criticism, freedom to think and speak are not self-evident necessities. It is only from the hope and the intention of discovering truth that freedom acquires such high public

significance. . . . The right to utter words, whether or not they have meaning, and regardless of their truth, could not be a vital interest of a great state but for the presumption that they are the chaff which goes with the utterance of true and significant words.

Our greatest need today is not to shove back ever farther the boundaries of free speech, but to remember why speech matters at all. We shall then recognize that not everything that can be called speech or expression really does matter.

"Without [freedom of expression], other fundamental rights, like the right to vote, would wither and die."

Limits Should Not Be Placed on Freedom of Expression

American Civil Liberties Union

In the following viewpoint the American Civil Liberties Union (ACLU) argues that protecting free expression is essential to maintaining a free society. According to the ACLU, the First Amendment protects "pure speech"—spoken and printed materials—and "symbolic speech"—nonverbal expression that includes flag burning and works of art. The ACLU maintains that even unpopular forms of expression, such as hate speech, should be protected to ensure the free flow of ideas. The ACLU is a nonprofit agency that protects civil rights and civil liberties.

As you read, consider the following questions:

1. As noted by the author, why was Sidney Street jailed in 1969?
2. What is the "Brandenberg standard," according to the author?
3. As stated by the ACLU, what kind of political protest does the First Amendment not protect?

American Civil Liberties Union, "Freedom of Expression," *ACLU Briefing Paper*, 1997. Copyright © 1997 by the American Civil Liberties Union. Reproduced by permission.

Freedom of speech, of the press, of association, of assembly and petition—this set of guarantees, protected by the First Amendment, comprises what we refer to as freedom of expression. The Supreme Court has written that this freedom is "the matrix, the indispensable condition of nearly every other form of freedom." Without it, other fundamental rights, like the right to vote, would wither and die.

But in spite of its "preferred position" in our constitutional hierarchy, the nation's commitment to freedom of expression has been tested over and over again. Especially during times of national stress, like war abroad or social upheaval at home, people exercising their First Amendment rights have been censored, fined, even jailed. Those with unpopular political ideas have always borne the brunt of government repression. It was during WWI—hardly ancient history—that a person could be jailed just for giving out anti-war leaflets. Out of those early cases, modern First Amendment law evolved. Many struggles and many cases later, ours is the most speech-protective country in the world.

The path to freedom was long and arduous. It took nearly 200 years to establish firm constitutional limits on the government's power to punish "seditious" and "subversive" speech. Many people suffered along the way, such as labor leader Eugene V. Debs, who was sentenced to 10 years in prison under the Espionage Act just for telling a rally of peaceful workers to realize they were "fit for something better than slavery and cannon fodder." Or Sidney Street, jailed in 1969 for burning an American flag on a Harlem street corner to protest the shooting of civil rights figure James Meredith.

Free speech rights still need constant, vigilant protection. New questions arise and old ones return. Should flag burning be a crime? What about government or private censorship of works of art that touch on sensitive issues like religion or sexuality? Should the Internet be subject to any form of government control? What about punishing college students who espouse racist or sexist opinions? In answering these questions, the history and the core values of the First Amendment should be our guide.

The Supreme Court and the First Amendment

During our nation's early era, the courts were almost universally hostile to political minorities' First Amendment rights; free speech issues did not even reach the Supreme Court until 1919 when, in *Schenck v. U.S.*, the Court unanimously upheld the conviction of a Socialist Party member for mailing leaflets to draft-age men. A turning point occurred a few months later in *Abrams v. U.S.* Although the defendant's conviction under the Espionage Act for distributing anti-war leaflets was upheld, two dissenting opinions formed the cornerstone of our modern First Amendment law. Justices Oliver Wendell Holmes and Louis D. Brandeis argued speech could *only* be punished *if* it presented "a clear and present danger" of imminent harm. Mere political advocacy, they said, was protected by the First Amendment. Eventually, these justices were able to convince a majority of the Court to adopt the "clear and present danger test."

From then on, the right to freedom of expression grew more secure—until the 1950s and McCarthyism.[1] The Supreme Court fell prey to the witchhunt mentality of that period, seriously weakening the "clear and present danger" test by holding that speakers could be punished if they advocated overthrowing the government—even if the danger of such an occurrence were both slight and remote. As a result, many political activists were prosecuted and jailed simply for advocating communist revolution. Loyalty oath requirements for government employees were upheld; thousands of Americans lost their jobs on the basis of flimsy evidence supplied by secret witnesses.

Finally, in 1969, in *Brandenberg v. Ohio*, the Supreme Court struck down the conviction of a Ku Klux Klan member, and established a new standard: Speech can be suppressed only if it is intended, *and likely to produce*, "imminent lawless action." Otherwise, even speech that advocates violence is protected. The Brandenberg standard prevails today.

1. In the 1950s Senator Joseph McCarthy accused large numbers of U.S. officials of being Communists. His charges were never proven, and he was censured by the Senate in 1954.

What Does "Protected Speech" Include?

First Amendment protection is not limited to "pure speech"—books, newspapers, leaflets, and rallies. It also protects "symbolic speech"—nonverbal expression whose purpose is to communicate ideas. In its 1969 decision in *Tinker v. Des Moines*, the Court recognized the right of public school students to wear black armbands in protest of the Vietnam War. In 1989 (*Texas v. Johnson*) and again in 1990 (*U.S. v. Eichman*), the Court struck down government bans on "flag desecration." Other examples of protected symbolic speech include works of art, T-shirt slogans, political buttons, music lyrics and theatrical performances.

Government can limit some protected speech by imposing "time, place and manner" restrictions. This is most commonly done by requiring permits for meetings, rallies and demonstrations. But a permit cannot be unreasonably withheld, nor can it be denied based on content of the speech. That would be what is called viewpoint discrimination—and *that* is unconstitutional.

When a protest crosses the line from speech to action, the government can intervene more aggressively. Political protesters have the right to picket, to distribute literature, to chant and to engage passersby in debate. But they do not have the right to block building entrances or to physically harass people.

Free Speech for Hatemongers?

The ACLU [American Civil Liberties Union] has often been at the center of controversy for defending the free speech rights of groups that spew hate, such as the Ku Klux Klan and the Nazis. But if only popular ideas were protected, we wouldn't need a First Amendment. History teaches that the first target of government repression is never the last. If we do not come to the defense of the free speech rights of the most unpopular among us, even if their views are antithetical to the very freedom the First Amendment stands for, then no one's liberty will be secure. In that sense, all First Amendment rights are "indivisible."

Censoring so-called hate speech also runs counter to the long-term interests of the most frequent victims of hate:

racial, ethnic, religious and sexual minorities. We should not give the government the power to decide which opinions are hateful, for history has taught us that government is more apt to use this power to prosecute minorities than to protect them. As one federal judge has put it, tolerating hateful speech is "the best protection we have against any Nazi-type regime in this country."

Three Reasons Why Freedom of Expression Is Essential to a Free Society

• It's the foundation of self-fulfillment. The right to express one's thoughts and to communicate freely with others affirms the dignity and worth of each and every member of society, and allows each individual to realize his or her full human potential. Thus, freedom of expression is an end in itself—and as such, deserves society's greatest protection.

• It's vital to the attainment and advancement of knowledge, and the search for the truth. The eminent 19th-century writer and civil libertarian, John Stuart Mill, contended that enlightened judgment is possible only if one considers all facts and ideas, from whatever source, and tests one's own conclusions against opposing views. Therefore, all points of view—even those that are "bad" or socially harmful—should be represented in society's "marketplace of ideas."

• It's necessary to our system of self-government and gives the American people a "checking function" against government excess and corruption. If the American people are to be the masters of their fate and of their elected government, they must be well-informed and have access to all information, ideas and points of view. Mass ignorance is a breeding ground for oppression and tyranny.

American Civil Liberties Union, "Freedom of Expression," 1997.

At the same time, freedom of speech does not prevent punishing conduct that intimidates, harasses, or threatens another person, even if words are used. Threatening phone calls, for example, are not constitutionally protected.

Speech and National Security

The Supreme Court has recognized the government's interest in keeping some information secret, such as wartime troop deployments. But the Court has never actually upheld an injunction against speech on national security grounds. Two lessons can be learned from this historical fact. First, the amount of speech that can be curtailed in the interest of national security is very limited. And second, the government has historically overused the concept of "national security" to shield itself from criticism, and to discourage public discussion of controversial policies or decisions.

In 1971, the publication of the "Pentagon Papers" by the *New York Times* brought the conflicting claims of free speech and national security to a head. "The Pentagon Papers," a voluminous secret history and analysis of the country's involvement in Vietnam, was leaked to the press. When the *Times* ignored the government's demand that it cease publication, the stage was set for a Supreme Court decision. In the landmark *U.S. v. New York Times* case, the Court ruled that the government could not, through "prior restraint," block publication of any material unless it could prove that it would "surely" result in "direct, immediate, and irreparable" harm to the nation. This the government failed to prove, and the public was given access to vital information about an issue of enormous importance.

The public's First Amendment "right to know" is essential to its ability to fully participate in democratic decision-making. As the "Pentagon Papers" case demonstrates, the government's claims of "national security" must always be closely scrutinized to make sure they are valid.

Unprotected Expression

The Supreme Court has recognized several limited exceptions to First Amendment protection.

- In *Chaplinsky v. New Hampshire* (1942), the Court held that so-called "fighting words . . . which by their very utterance inflict injury or tend to incite an immediate breach of the peace," are not protected. This decision was based on the fact that fighting words are of "slight social value as a step to truth."
- In *New York Times Co. v. Sullivan* (1964), the Court held that defamatory falsehoods about public officials can be punished—*only* if the offended official can prove the falsehoods were published with "actual malice," i.e.:

"knowledge that the statement was false or with reckless disregard of whether it was false or not." Other kinds of "libelous statements" are also punishable.

- Legally "obscene" material has historically been excluded from First Amendment protection. Unfortunately, the relatively narrow obscenity exception, described below, has been abused by government authorities and private pressure groups. Sexual expression in art and entertainment is, and has historically been, the most frequent target of censorship crusades, from James Joyce's classic *Ulysses* to the photographs of Robert Mapplethorpe.

In the 1973 *Miller v. California* decision, the Court established three conditions that must be present if a work is to be deemed "legally obscene." It must 1) appeal to the average person's prurient (shameful, morbid) interest in sex; 2) depict sexual conduct in a "patently offensive way" as defined by community standards; and 3) taken as a whole, lack serious literary, artistic, political or scientific value. Attempts to apply the "Miller test" have demonstrated the impossibility of formulating a precise definition of obscenity. Justice Potter Stewart once delivered a famous one-liner on the subject: "I know it when I see it." But the fact is, the obscenity exception to the First Amendment is highly subjective and practically invites government abuse.

The ACLU: Ongoing Champion of Free Expression

The American Civil Liberties Union has been involved in virtually all of the landmark First Amendment cases to reach the U.S. Supreme Court, and remains absolutely committed to the preservation of each and every individual's freedom of expression. During the 1980s, we defended the right of artists and entertainers to perform and produce works of art free of government and private censorship. During the 1990s, the organization fought to protect free speech in cyberspace when state and federal government attempted to impose content-based regulations on the Internet. In addition, the ACLU offers several books on the subject of freedom of expression.

"It may be worth considering some very limited restrictions on some hate expression."

Hate Speech Should Be Regulated

Laura Leets

According to Laura Leets in the following viewpoint, some limits should be placed on hate speech because it may contribute to the incidence of hate crimes. Although hate speech usually does not have immediate consequences, it may eventually combine with other influences to incite people to commit hate crimes, she argues. Moreover, she contends that many racist or other extremist groups are communicating their messages of hate to unprecedented numbers of people via the Internet. Public officials should consider enacting restrictions on hateful expressions, particularly those communicated over the Internet, to minimize the effects of racism and hatred in society, Leets maintains. Leets is an assistant professor in the communications department at Stanford University.

As you read, consider the following questions:

1. As explained by the author, what is the difference between "deterministic causality" and "probabilistic causality"?
2. What is moral exclusion, as defined by Susan Opotow?
3. Why would regulating hate speech on the Internet be difficult, according to Leets?

Laura Leets, "Should All Speech Be Free?" *The Quill*, vol. 89, May 2001, p. 38. Copyright © 2001 by the Society of Professional Journalists. Reproduced by permission of the author.

There's been a groundswell in the past several years to increase diversity in journalism, both in news coverage and in newsroom staffing. The goal of several diversity initiatives is to increase the number of voices that regularly appear in our newspapers, magazines, broadcasts and Web sites. It's important to seek different perspectives and ideas, and the goal of such initiatives is an admirable and productive one. There are some voices, however, that have demonstrably adverse effects. So while the journalism community, judicial system and American public generally support tolerance of diverse viewpoints, some perspectives and types of speech still warrant concern.

The Rising Incidence of Hate Crimes

One problematic voice is that of hate. Whether it is the dragging death of an African-American behind a pick-up truck in Texas, a gay student's murder in Wyoming, a racially motivated shooting spree at a Los Angeles Jewish community center or a bloody rampage by two high school students enamored of Hitler's fascism, the rising incidence of hate crimes and the groups who appear to encourage them is attracting public interest.[1] In particular, the World Wide Web has provided marginalized extremist groups a more notable and accessible public platform. The Internet has put the problem of incendiary hate into sharp relief.

In several research studies where I have focused on short-term message effects of hate speech, it is difficult to demonstrate with certainty the linkage between hate expression and violence or harm (deterministic causality). In a recent study, I asked 266 participants (both university and non-university students recruited online) to read and evaluate one of 11 white supremacist Web pages that I had randomly sampled from the Internet. Similar to previous studies, the data showed that the content of the hate Web pages was per-

---

1. In 1998 African-American James Byrd was chained to a pick-up truck and dragged to death. Gay college student Matthew Shepard was beaten and then tied to a post and left to die in Wyoming in 1998. In 1999 Buford O'Neal Furrow entered a Jewish Community Center in Los Angeles and opened fire, wounding five people, including three young children. At Columbine High School in Colorado in 1999, students Eric Harris and Dylan Klebold went on a shooting rampage, killing fifteen and wounding twenty-three others.

ceived to be in keeping with the Court bounds for First Amendment protection. Yet the participants acknowledged an indirect effect that, on the other hand, may suggest hate speech effects are more slow-acting—and thus imperceptible in the short term (probabilistic causality).

Specifically, participants in the cyberhate study rated the indirect threats from the World Church of the Creator (WCOTC) [a white supremacist organization] Web page as very high (Mean=6, on a seven-point scale where seven represented the highest score). Is it coincidental that a former WCOTC member . . . shot 11 Asian Americans, African-Americans and Jews, killing two, before committing suicide? Or that two brothers associated with WCOTC were charged with murdering a gay couple and fire-bombing three Sacramento synagogues? While WCOTC leader Matthew Hale does not endorse this lawlessness, neither does he condemn it. Part of their ideology is that all nonwhites are "mud people," people without souls, like animals eligible for harm.

The Real Harm

Current legal remedies may be missing the real harm of racist indoctrination, which may not be immediately apparent or verifiable. For instance, hate expressions tend to encourage a set of beliefs that develop gradually and that often can lie dormant until conditions are ripe for a climate of moral exclusion and subsequent crimes against humanity. Moral exclusion is defined by Susan Opotow, an independent scholar affiliated with Teachers College at Columbia University, as the psychosocial orientation toward individuals or groups for whom justice principles or considerations of fairness are not applicable. People who are morally excluded are perceived as nonentities, and harming them appears acceptable and just (e.g., slavery, holocaust).

It is not the abstract viewpoints that are problematic. Rather, it is the expressions intending to elicit persecution or oppression that often begin with dehumanizing rhetoric. In my research, I argue that communication is the primary means by which psychological distancing occurs. Arguably, it may be the long-term, not short-term, effects of hate expression that are potentially more far reaching.

Examining the Internet

Even though prevailing First Amendment dogma maintains that speech may not be penalized merely because its content is racist, sexist or basically abhorrent, Internet law is a dynamic area and as such is not completely integrated into our regulatory and legal system. Consequently, many questions remain about how traditional laws should apply to this new and unique medium.

The Internet can combine elements of print (newspapers and magazines), broadcast (television and radio) and face-to-face interaction. Moreover, unlike users of previous media, those on the Internet have the power to reach a mass audience, but in this case the audience must be more active in seeking information, as cyberspace is less intrusive than other mass media.

Exceptions to the First Amendment

Rules against hate speech, homophobic remarks and misogyny serve both symbolic and institutional values—increasing productivity in the workplace and protecting a learning environment on campus. It has been argued that such prohibitions operate in derogation of the First Amendment's guarantee of freedom of speech, but that amendment already is subject to dozens of exceptions—libel, defamation, words of conspiracy or threat, disrespectful words uttered to a judge or police officer, irrelevant or untrue words spoken in a judicial proceeding, copyright, plagiarism, official secrets, misleading advertising and many more. The social interest in deterring vicious racial or sexual vituperation certainly seems at least as great as that underlying these other forms of speech deemed unworthy of First Amendment protection.

Richard Delgado, *Insight on the News*, June 24, 1996.

It is unclear whether content-based restrictions found in other technological media may be permissible for the Internet. For example, the FCC [Federal Communications Commission] ruled that indecency was unsuitable for broadcast media because of ease of access, invasiveness and spectrum scarcity, yet cable and print media are not subjected to this form of content regulation.

In 1996, the United States Congress passed the Telecommunications Bill, which included the Communications Decency Act (CDA). The CDA regulated indecent or obscene material for adults on the Internet, applying First Amendment jurisprudence from broadcast and obscenity cases. Later that year, the Supreme Court declared two provisions unconstitutional in *Reno vs. ACLU*. Congress and the Court disagreed on the medium-specific constitutional speech standard suitable for the World Wide Web. Congress argued that the Internet should be regulated in the same manner as television or radio, but the Court decided not to apply that doctrinal framework. Instead, the Court viewed the Internet as face-to-face communication, deserving full protection.

Is Regulation Possible?

Issues of Internet regulation naturally lead to the question of whether such regulation is even possible. Cyberspace doesn't have geographical boundaries, so it is difficult to determine where violations of the law should be prosecuted. There are enforcement conflicts, not only between different countries' legal jurisdictions, but also among federal, state and local levels in the United States. Although Americans place a high premium on free expression, without much effort most people can find Internet material that they would want to censor.

Some argue that cyberhate oversteps this idea of "mere insult" and warrants liability. The Internet is a powerful forum of communication with its broad (world-wide) reach, interactivity and multi-media capability to disseminate information. These features inevitably result in concerns about impact, especially when viewed as empowering racists and other extremists. It is common for people to wonder whether white supremacist Web pages cause hate crime. This question is similar to people's concerns regarding whether TV violence causes aggression in viewers. The issue of causation (claim: x causes y) is an important one to address.

It is important to differentiate between language determining (or causing) an effect and language influencing the probability of an effect. In terms of a strict social science approach (deterministic causation) we can't say language has an effect unless three conditions are met: (a) there must be a relationship between the hypothesized cause and the observed effect, (b) the cause must always precede the effect in time (x must come before y), and (c) all alternative explanations for the effect must be eliminated. The problem with making a strong case for a causal effect lies with the second and third conditions. For example, most media (television, Internet etc.) effects are probabilistic, not deterministic. It is almost impossible to make a clear case for television or cyberhate effects because the relationship is almost never a simple causal one. Instead, there are many factors in the influence process. Each factor increases the probability of an effect occurring. The effects process is complex.

The U.S. Supreme Court has traditionally viewed speech effects in terms of short-term, deterministic consequences, and has not considered more far-reaching effects.

While more research is needed on the long-term effects of hate speech, it may be worth considering some very limited restrictions on some hate expression. American jurisprudence has not fully realized the harmful nature and effects stemming from hate speech, which has the ability both to directly elicit immediate behavior (short term) and to cultivate an oppressive climate (long term).

"*Hate speech is the very essence of free speech.*"

Hate Speech Should Not Be Regulated

Ted Gup

Ted Gup, a journalism professor at Case Western Reserve University in Cleveland, Ohio, argues in the following viewpoint that free expression of hate speech is essential to reducing bigotry in society. He contends that hatred and racism flourish when open debate is discouraged. Allowing open discussion of hateful ideas is the best way to invite opposing voices that discredit prejudice and encourage tolerance, in the author's opinion.

As you read, consider the following questions:
1. What incident clarified the difference between speech and action for the author?
2. As quoted by Gup, what is Abe Ayad's goal?
3. According to Gup, what reaction do symbols of hate elicit in society?

Ted Gup, "At the Corner of Hate and Free Speech," *Washington Post*, December 15, 2002, p. B1. Copyright © 2002 by the Washington Post Book World Service/ Washington Post Writers Group. Reproduced by permission of the author.

I would like to have lunch at Grandpa's Kitchen, a convenience store and deli on East 55th and Chester [in Cleveland, Ohio]. But despite its warm and fuzzy name, I fear that I would not be entirely welcome there. I say this because of the huge mural on the side of the building that depicts Jews as monkeys wearing yarmulkes. The owner, a Mr. Brahim "Abe" Ayad, has made it pretty clear that he is none too fond of people of my faith. He has his reasons, many of them involving his father, a Palestinian who he says was driven from his land to make way for the state of Israel. Today, Grandpa's Kitchen is a kind of local landmark, a testament to unmuzzled anti-Semitism. But the fact that this animosity has been allowed to fester publicly is one that I, the grandson of a rabbi, applaud without reservation.

I am drawn to Grandpa's Kitchen because it is contested ground between those who argue that they have a right to be rid of such venomous expression and those who say it is a vital exercise of free speech. It is a debate being carried on not only on this seedy Cleveland corner but also by the Supreme Court, which [in 2002] heard arguments on whether cross burning should be considered protected free speech.[1]

Even Harvard Law School, where generations of students have been trained to defend the First Amendment, [considered] a speech code targeted at the lexicon of hate [in 2002]. In this it is hardly alone. Corporations, clubs, elementary schools and universities have convinced themselves that the enlightened thing to do is to declare that "Hate speech is not free speech," to quote Robert A. Corrigan, the president of San Francisco State University.

I believe they are not only wrong but dangerously wrong. Any effort to stifle hate speech is a betrayal of democratic values—the very ones that ultimately protect diversity and dissent. It seems to me that unfettered speech is to bigotry what a vaccine is to smallpox.

---

1. In *Virginia v. Black* in 2002, the Supreme Court decided that states could lawfully ban the burning of crosses as a means of intimidation or harassment. The case was brought by two men, Richard J. Elliott and Jonathan O'Mara, who were convicted by Virginia law of setting fire to a cross in an African American man's yard. A state court overturned the verdict, but the Supreme Court reversed the decision, upholding the Virginia law.

Sticks and Stones

I understand the emotional appeal of speech codes, and I well know how noxious and hurtful words can be. As a Jew growing up in Ohio in the 1950s, I was branded a "shylock" and a "kike." I was threatened and, on occasion, beaten. In junior high, two classmates stabbed me with a pencil, and four decades later, two graphite points are still plainly visible in my left hand. That helped clarify for me the difference between speech and action, or the "sticks and stones" rule of the playground. Today my sons, adopted from South Korea, also know that words can be ugly. I listen in pained silence as they tell me of classmates who taunt them by pinching the corners of their own eyes or call them "chinks." Over a soda, I tell my son who gets off the yellow school bus with a black eye that I understand, even if I can't explain what fuels his tormenters.

But as a journalist and as an American, I feel a curious, almost perverse, sense of pride that Grandpa's Kitchen, with its notorious mural, could find a secure place in this city of immigrants and minorities. Beyond that, I have a feeling that Abe (as I have begun to think of him) may have something to teach me and that I owe him—no, I owe myself—a visit. And so I call him at the deli, identify myself as both a journalist and a Jew, and ask if his door is open to me. "I'm open to all good people," he says with such warmth that I am left almost speechless. "Thanks," I hear myself say. "Look forward to meeting you." (Did I really say that?) "All right, brother," he says. Brother?

On a scrap of paper, I jot down—"Monday/Lunch/Grandpa's Kitchen"—as if I might forget.

The first thing I see as I pull up to the deli is the mural, a pastiche of offensive images and accusations. One depicts a Jewish conspiracy in control of American network television. Another shows Jesus Christ in agony on the cross. Just inside the door, a news article is tacked to the wall: "Tel Aviv Mayor Seeks Help in Cleveland." Above it is written "Proof Implicating Jews." Am I not now in hostile territory?

I have a pretty good idea of what Abe will be like—crude, mean-spirited, not too smart. But the man well-known for the past several years for his offensive murals approaches me in a white apron and extends a huge hand. He is courtly, soft-spoken and oddly vulnerable. He offers me a cup of coffee and puts a fresh pot on to brew. At 36, he is a big man, 6-foot-1, 250 pounds. His eyes are hidden behind gold-rimmed sunglasses. He seems as curious about me as I am about him. There are no tables or chairs, only a takeout counter, so he stacks plastic milk crates in the aisle should we want to sit.

Challenging Stereotypes

I had expected someone consumed with hate and at first he confirms my stereotype. He hands me a book entitled "The Ugly Truth About the ADL [Anti-Defamation League]." He calls [the terrorist attacks on September 11, 2001] a Jewish conspiracy and produces a poster depicting Israeli leaders astride missiles labeled "Nuke" and "Chemical." Their target is spelled out: "Islam World or Bust."

But if he is a bigot he is most selective. A moment earlier, the poster was hidden behind a painting celebrating Black History Month, a work done at his expense and featuring Malcolm X and Jesse Jackson and others. Elsewhere are certificates recording his contributions to a Baptist church (he is a Muslim), to George Washington Carver Elementary and to an organization for foster children. Maybe, I tell myself, he's just a shrewd businessman ingratiating himself with the African American community. But he seems so earnest. Most of his patrons are black, and he greets them with a hug and calls them "Brother."

His menu also reflects a certain ecumenicalism: gyros, Polish Boy sausages, catfish and okra, and a Reuben (What Jewish deli would be without?).

I have come to find out who Abe is and what he wants. The answer to each is the same. He is the son of a Palestinian who immigrated to the United States in 1926 and whose service to the U.S. Army in World War II left him disabled, he says.

Abe was born in Dearborn, Mich. At 6, he and his family moved back to the West Bank. At 8, he says, he was on his way to school when an Israeli soldier shot him with a rubber bullet. At my request, he rolls up his pant leg to show me the dime-sized scar on his knee. He says he was also shot in the rump. We both laugh as he declines to proffer the evidence.

That same day, he says, two of his friends were shot dead.

"How do you like your coffee?" he asks.

What is it, I ask him, that he hopes to accomplish with his attacks on Jews? "It should be perceived as a plea for help," he says. "I'm not going to hurt anybody. That is not even an option." He adds, "I just want to vent my frustrations and my disappointments. How else could I get their attention?" And then there is his quixotic effort to win back lands he says were his father's and are his rightful inheritance, land on which, he says, there are now Jewish settlements and factories. "ALL I WANT IS MY LAND" is painted on the mural. "I just want justice. I can't ask for revenge—that's God's. I'm just trying to break the cycle of hate that's been consuming us."

Asay. © by Creators Syndicate. Reprinted with permission.

But how can he expect to promote understanding while using words of hate? How misguided, I think. He is also critical of the Palestinian government and suicide bombers. "We're at fault just as much because we're targeting innocent people," he says. Hurting anyone is "the last thing I'm trying to do."

He is a father of eight. I ask him what lessons he teaches

his children. "I tell them to stand up for what's right. Don't let anybody step on anybody and don't step on anybody. You don't have to be afraid of anybody. Not here. Never here." Not so different from what I tell my own sons.

Hidden Prejudice

The landscape of my youth had no such murals of intolerance. Instead, prejudice was hidden behind disingenuous smiles and behind the manicured hedges of off-limits country clubs and the ivied walls of universities with secret quotas. As a boy in Canton, Ohio, I remember my family fantasized about living beside a lake on the edge of town, but we knew it was closed to "our kind." The word that was used, if it was uttered at all, was "restricted." How antiseptic.

The year Abe was born, I was attending a Midwest boarding school where I suffered overt anti-Semitism from some of my classmates. But I also suspected that the school itself was complicit. I felt unwelcome and inadequate. For years, I wondered whether I was just paranoid. Then, two decades after graduation, I was invited to return as a "distinguished" guest-lecturer. That was when I got a glimpse of my student file. There, on the outside jacket, was a Star of David and a tiny notation that suggested that perhaps in the future, local fathers might screen out such applicants.

The note didn't upset me as much as it brought a sense of relief that my suspicions were being confirmed. If only I and others of my generation had had the opportunity to confront the authors of such notes. If only they had spoken their objections and aired their biases publicly. Why in the world would we now, in the name of speech codes, want to drive them back into the safety of their secret lairs?

Speech codes threaten to take us back to the old days when prejudice was vented only in whispers between like minds. My own history has convinced me that a silenced bigot can do far more mischief than one who airs his hatred publicly.

The Best Defense

From my parents I learned the difference between the acute sting of an ethnic slur and the anguish of a polite cold shoulder. Years ago, a clerk at a fashionable Virginia Beach hotel discreetly asked my parents about our family name, then turned them away into the night. They were on their honeymoon. That was 1947, the year the movie "Gentleman's Agreement" captured the silent complicity upon which anti-Semitism—indeed all bigotry—depends. The other evening I lent the film to an African American neighbor. He returned it the next morning shaking his head and told me about his own experience. Working through a team of lawyers, only weeks before he had been close to buying a company. Then the owners discovered he was black. The price tripled. The deal fell through. Nothing uncivil was ever said, but it seldom is. That's why I defend Abe's right to express his hostilities. I see it as my own best defense.

Don't get me wrong. The murals make me cringe, but I much prefer that his feelings be out in the open. They tell me where I stand with Abe. They also invite the possibility, however slim, that we might find some sliver of common ground, that confrontation could lead to conciliation.

Even the most reviled of hate symbols, the burning cross and the swastika, are just that—emblems of unspeakable evil. But their sporadic resurfacing has produced not waves of terror but waves of public revulsion, not Kristallnachts[2] and lynchings but community rallies against racism. Hate speech need not be a precursor to violence. On the contrary, it can defuse tensions that could turn explosive. Hate speech can discredit nascent movements that might otherwise draw strength from authoritarian efforts to snuff them out. Intimidation invites intimidation.

Speech codes empower the impotent. I wince when I hear raw ethnic, racial and sexual slurs. But even worse is the notion that people who think that way could move about among us, unknown and unchallenged. "You can't cure it if you can't hear it," my mother says. She's right. Bigotry is an affliction not of the mouth but of the mind.

And while free speech often causes pain, it also holds out the only real promise of progress. In the end, like it or not,

---

2. *Kristallnacht*, meaning the "night of broken glass," is the name given to acts of vandalism by Nazi youths committed against Jewish property on a night in Vienna in 1939.

hate speech is the very essence of free speech and its airing is and always has been a potent self-corrective. This is what Abe may be able to teach Harvard Law.

Opening a Dialogue

I have no illusion that my visit with Abe changed his mind about Jews or put out years of smoldering resentment, but it did open a dialogue and, humble as that may be, it is a start. Not long before, a . . . columnist, Regina Brett, did something similar by suggesting a new use for a billboard next to Grandpa's Kitchen. Today, in red letters two feet high it declares: "The Hate Stops Here." It may be an opening salvo. The feelings Abe has stirred have triggered something larger—a community campaign against bigotry.

I ask him what he thinks of the sign, expecting him to denounce it. "'The Hate Stops Here.' I hope it does." He adds proudly, "That's my sign. That's my message. I mean look at what one man can do—me." Once more he's left me speechless. "Let's make sure the hate stops here," he says, "and not just sweep it under the rug. Let's resolve it like human beings."

Well, maybe the hate doesn't quite stop here—not yet anyway, but maybe someday.

> "Without a measure of legal protection the flag is devalued . . . and destined to disappear."

Flag Desecration Should Be Restricted

Shawntel Smith

In the following viewpoint Shawntel Smith attempts to persuade Congress to enact an amendment that would protect the American flag from desecration. She contends that the flag symbolizes the values that make America great: freedom, opportunity, and unity. Desecrating the flag, she argues, essentially rejects the values that the flag represents. The proposed amendment was defeated in 1999. Smith is a former Miss America winner.

As you read, consider the following questions:
1. What is the "American dream," as defined by the author?
2. In Smith's opinion, why is the American flag unique?
3. According to Smith, why is desecrating the flag not protected as free speech?

Shawntel Smith, testimony before the U.S. House of Representatives, Washington, DC, March 23, 1999.

M r. Chairman, members of the House Judiciary Sub-committee, my name is Shawntel Smith and I proudly call Muldrow, Oklahoma my home. It is an honor to speak to each of you today in support of House Joint Resolution 33, a proposed constitutional amendment that would restore the Flag of the United States of America to its proper place of honor.[1]

I, like many others, have had family members serve in the military. They served very courageously and proudly. Just to name a few, my Great-grandfather Powell served in the Civil War. My Grandfather Fouts—Roy Gideon Fouts—served as Seaman First Class in World War II. My Grandpa Smith—Harold Elmo Smith—served as a supply Sergeant in World War II and was on one of the first waves onto the beaches of Normandy. And my father Gailen Maurice Smith served as a Sergeant in the National Guard. I have great pride that my family has contributed to preserving the freedoms that our great nation stands for, and the symbol of that freedom, the United States Flag.

The American Dream

I count myself fortunate as one of but a few American women to have conferred upon them the title of "Miss America." As the 75th Miss America, I traveled some 20,000 miles a month sharing the message of STW [School-To-Work] Reinventing America's Work Force. I visited 48 states and encouraged young people to develop skills, set goals, dream dreams and to become all they wish to become. I continue to share this message as Ambassador for the U.S. Departments of Education and Labor. I also share with young people that life is not about fairy tales but that it is about never giving up, never giving in and overcoming obstacles that may arise. I believe in the American Dream—which is the freedom to achieve greatness through hard work, perseverance and determination.

I believe, as I stated earlier, that our flag is the symbol of the American Dream. I can remember standing in elementary school and saying the Pledge of Allegiance. And, today, I love

1. The proposed flag desecration amendment was defeated in the Senate.

51

watching the little boy or girl reciting the Pledge of Allegiance at the top of their lungs. Young people that say the Pledge of Allegiance with such boldness view the flag as a cornerstone—one of strength, safety and opportunity. I am constantly amazed at the reverence it receives from our youngest Americans. Children exhibit special concern . . . to treat it reverently, to stand tall and proud as they recite the Pledge of Allegiance.

It was brought to my attention not too long ago, indeed, most Americans would be shocked to learn that today it is okay, not illegal, to desecrate the symbol of our nation, the symbol of hope for the world's people—the American Flag. In fact [of] those who were informed about the current law, or lack of a protecting law, 80% favored an amendment to the constitution that would provide legal protection of Old Glory.

Restoring the Star Spangled Banner

Not far from Capitol Hill, in the Museum of American History, a project is underway to restore the Star Spangled Banner, the 15-star, 15-stripe flag that is THE symbol of determination for a free people. It is one flag around which our nation now begins to rally in order to preserve and protect us as we move into the new millennium. Part of a government program to preserve national treasures, more than $5 million will be dedicated to its preservation.

There are two interesting points, among many, about this particular flag: it is the largest historic textile in the world, and is one of invaluable historic significance. In short, it is a piece of cloth that reminds us of our heritage—as is, as does, every American Flag.

We might ask: is the Star Spangled Banner of 1814 THE flag of the United States? Yes and No. There were other similar flags before, and many others that came later, each of which [was] and still [is] THE flag of the United States.

Some might argue that burning "A" flag is different from burning "THE" flag of 1814. Our flag, however, is unique in that it exists only in copies and, therefore, every flag is THE flag. If we recognize the need to preserve and protect the Star Spangled Banner, then we should recognize the value and need in the preservation and protection of all Star Spangled Banners.

The Star Spangled Banner in the museum is, physically, less than the one we might envision. Over the years, well meaning Americans have clipped portions off as souvenirs, or awards, with no regard to the importance of keeping the flag whole. Had his practice gone unchecked, the Star Spangled Banner would be but a memory.

Justifiable Limitations on the First Amendment

Many well-meaning folks contend that if we prohibit the desecration of our flag, we do harm to our right to free speech secured by the First Amendment. While I understand these feelings, I disagree with them. I do not believe that the burning or desecration of our flag constitutes speech. It is conduct. As such, the First Amendment has no application to flag desecration, because the First Amendment protects only speech.

Even if flag burning and the like could be considered a form of speech, the First Amendment should not reach this manner of speech. The First Amendment is not absolute. For instance, there is no First Amendment right to yell fire in a theater or to provoke others through fighting words. The flag occupies such a critical, unique place in our nation's life that its desecration amounts to "fighting words" for many. For the reasons I set forth above, I believe that another justifiable limitation on the First Amendment is the protection of our national symbol, Old Glory.

John N. Hostettler, "Position on a Constitutional Amendment Prohibiting Flag Desecration," July 3, 2002.

Those who oppose legal protection, well meaning as they may be, relegate the flag of the United States to the same fate. Without a measure of legal protection the flag is devalued, figuratively "clipped" and destined to disappear.

Embodying America

The flag of the United States flies today as it did over Fort McHenry. And today, just as it did then, it embodies what we think of as America and it causes us to pause and remember what and who got us here.

The memory of Americans who gave their lives is woven in every stitch of the flag, no matter its size or age. And, whether it flew over Ft. McHenry, over the US Capitol, or from the hand of a young child, the integrity of the flag of the United States deserves protection and preservation.

As we go to the millennium, we are looking back on our heritage with a deep concern for preserving those things uniquely American. The 106th Congress has the opportunity to be part of this preservation effort by providing our flag a measure of protection from desecration.

While the archives at the Museum mark the millennium by saving crumbling pieces of our heritage that are in danger of being lost, a flag protection amendment could do the same. It can limit the destructive actions of those who would literally rip the flag apart, causing it to crumble and committing it to history, ultimately lost as a "living" symbol of our great nation.

A Values Issue

Burning a flag is not a matter of free speech, but I believe it is a matter of behavior. It is an insult to the intelligence of the vast majority of common-sense Americans to call flag burning "speech." This is a values issue for the American people. America is a tapestry of diverse peoples. The uniqueness of our nation is our diversity. The flag represents the values, traditions and aspirations that bind us together as a nation. It stands above our differences and unites us in war and peace.

Because I was blessed with the position of Miss America, I had many unforgettable experiences. One in particular I would like to share with you today. Just after beginning my year of service I was asked by the Governor of Oklahoma, Governor Frank Keating, to participate in the Thank You America Tour—which gave thanks to all of those who so generously and bravely helped during the 1995 Oklahoma City bombing.[2] Being from Oklahoma I took great pride and felt such honor to participate in the ceremony at our nation's capital, Washington, DC. I remember walking into the war memorial room in which the ceremony was held; I was overwhelmed with emotion not only for the reason we were there but also because of what I saw. As I looked across the

2. In 1995 Timothy McVeigh bombed the Oklahoma City Federal Building, killing 168 people and injuring more than five hundred.

room, I saw flags from all the different countries and in the center of the room, there was a large United States flag. At that moment, I thought of all the men and women who fought for our country, many even sacrificed their lives. I was also reminded of how in a time of crisis we as Americans pull together to help one another.

I thank you for the opportunity to be here today and to share my concern for protecting the flag of the United States. I hope to have conveyed to you a few of the many meanings the United States flag embodies. Meanings of freedom, the American Dream, strength, security, opportunity, heritage and unity. To desecrate the flag would be to desecrate all that the flag stands for.

> "To forbid flag burning is to forbid you
> from disposing of your property in ways
> that offend others."

Flag Desecration Should Not Be Restricted

Andrew Cohen

According to Andrew Cohen in the following viewpoint, legislation prohibiting flag burning is unconstitutional. He contends that there is no one "American flag," there are only individually owned flags. Since flags are property, and because property rights are constitutionally protected, flag owners may burn their flags with impunity. The values that the flag symbolizes—self-determination and freedom from oppression—are not harmed by someone desecrating his or her own property, in Cohen's opinion. Cohen teaches philosophy at the University of Wisconsin, Stevens Point.

As you read, consider the following questions:
1. What does freedom of speech guarantee, according to the author?
2. When is the one time burning a flag should be against the law, in the author's opinion?
3. According to Cohen, for what did members of the armed services fight?

Andrew Cohen, "Flags, Flames, and Property," *Freeman*, vol. 49, January 1999, pp. 24–26. Copyright © 1999 by Foundation for Economic Education, Inc. Reproduced by permission.

A constitutional amendment that would forbid the desecration of American flags is again percolating in the nation's capital.[1] As of this writing [1999], the immediate prospects for passage look bleak. But this amendment has a way of never fully going away. Many opponents of the measure trot out free speech arguments. And although concerns about free expression are important, these traditional arguments miss a more central political principle that the amendment and resulting laws against flag burning would jeopardize: property rights. The amendment would undermine key liberties for which the flag stands.

Arguments for Flag Desecration Laws

Those who uphold laws against flag desecration typically speak of the important values that the flag symbolizes. They claim that legally allowing flag burning is tantamount to rejecting the freedoms that the flag represents. They say it is vital that we express our respect for human freedom by institutionalizing penalties against those who would defile the national symbol.

Permitting flag burning, the amendment's proponents continue, sends the wrong message to America's youth, America's voters, and observers abroad. When the young see protesters publicly burning a flag with impunity, they may believe that American freedoms are cheap. They may then think that the nation's commitment to uphold those freedoms is fleeting. Permitting flag burning may also undermine a key basis for community among America's voters. With protesters burning flags, voters may lose a vision of shared citizenship and be less committed to the American ideal. Flag burning is also supposedly a slap in the face to all Americans who suffered in wartime to secure freedoms for everyone. Lastly, foreign observers who see Americans burning their own flag may be less inclined to support America's international policies aimed at securing freedom. Advocates fear that foreigners will think: if Americans cannot take their own freedoms seriously, then we need not take seriously the moral reasoning they present to the world.

1. The proposed flag desecration amendment was defeated in 1999 in the Senate.

The Free Speech Argument Against Flag Desecration Laws

People who burn flags intend to send a message by doing so. This is what makes flag burning a form of expression. Some flag burners take offense at various American foreign policy measures. (Recall the nightly news broadcast [in 1998] showing Sudanese burning American flags in Khartoum after the United States bombed what it deemed a suspicious pharmaceutical factory.) Some individuals may burn flags as a way of saying America is not true to its own values. Others simply despise American ideals and set the flag aflame. In any case, people who burn flags do so deliberately in order to send a public message of protest.

The First Amendment to the Constitution reads, "Congress shall make no law . . . abridging the freedom of speech." Constitutional scholars and legal theorists have long argued over the meaning of this amendment. There is, however, a rough consensus on two ideas: (1) the amendment protects peaceful expression, popular or unpopular, but (2) the Framers clearly did not intend for it to license any and all forms of expression. Consequently, room has been made for laws against libel, slander, and obscenity. Contrary to hyperbolic op-eds railing against flaming protests, burning a flag is not "obscene." At worst, it is despicable. At best, it is a valuable form of political speech.

The First Amendment protects freedom of speech, which in turn protects the liberty to say wrong-headed, bigoted, stupid, vicious things. Such protection is crucial; otherwise freedom of speech would reduce to the empty freedom to say only the right, the true, and the good. That would present a disturbing practical difficulty: some bureaucrat would have to decide what is permissible speech, because in today's pluralistic society, there is little consensus on many aspects of the right, the true, and the good. Freedom of speech, however, is the freedom to say what one wishes without having to solicit the permission of anyone first.

Freedom of speech guarantees a healthy, open marketplace of ideas. More fundamentally, it includes the freedom to say things that others might not like. Those who are offended should respond with reasoned arguments of their own and not by passing a law. If individuals were only free to say things that others liked, public and private discussions would be banal, stilted, and oppressed. A law against flag burning forbids a form of expression simply because others do not like the message. Government exists, however, to protect individual rights. It should not protect citizens from being offended. We can stipulate that many acts of flag burning are offensive. Simply being offensive, however, does not violate individual rights.

The Property Rights Argument Against Flag Burning

The free speech argument against the proposed amendment is powerful; people must be free to offend if free speech is to count for anything. There is, however, one time when flag burning should be against the law: when it's someone else's flag.

Suppose you own a flag. Suppose that Chris takes your flag without your consent and sets it on fire in the public square. What Chris has done ought to be forbidden (and punished) not because he burned a flag, but because he burned your flag. Chris ought to be held accountable just as if he had taken a sledgehammer to your concrete garden gnomes without your permission. He destroyed your property.

The Rights of American Citizens

Banning flag desecration is an obvious and serious breach of the First Amendment and speech freedoms. We haven't seen protesters burning flags for the fun of it. When someone does this, they are making a serious political statement, which is, lo and behold, a guaranteed right of every U.S. citizen.

Anonymous, *Orange County Register*, July 23, 2001.

People who debate the flag issue often lose sight of this important fact: you cannot burn "the American flag" because there is no such thing as "the American flag." There are only flags. The "American flag" is an idea that cannot be burned. A particular flag, however, can be burned. Whether it is permissible to do so turns on whose flag it is.

Being a material object, a flag usually comes into the world attached to someone as property. A law against flag burning would forbid you from disposing of your property as you see fit. Let us assume that burning your flag does not pose a threat to public safety (that is, you don't ignite and toss it into an unsuspecting crowd). In that case, when you burn your flag, your actions are not importantly different from taking your paper and your ink to print up pamphlets that say anything (or even nothing) at all. The pamphlets are your property, and so too is your flag. Passersby can take your message or leave it.

To forbid flag burning is to forbid you from disposing of your property in ways that offend others. But property rights protect freedom of action for which one need not solicit the permission of others. A right to your flag guarantees a right to burn it, stomp on it, spit on it, or turn it into underwear if you so choose. Your flag is your property. If someone does not like what you do with your property, he should not lock you up; he should persuade you to change your ways or he should have nothing to do with you. Consider the absurdity of having rights to use your property only in ways others find acceptable.

Permissible Flag Burning and Some Problems

When a flag becomes old and tattered, there is a prescribed way to dispose of it. Part of the process involves burning it. If flag burning were forbidden, presumably it would not be just any flag burning that would be illegal. It would only be flag-burning-while-thinking-nasty-thoughts-about-the-flag. If persons are to be punished not for what they do, but for what they think, we will have marched a long way from the freedoms on which this nation was founded, and headed dangerously closer to tyranny.

There are further difficulties with laws against flag burning. We all know what an American flag is supposed to look like. It has 50 stars and 13 stripes, all arranged in a certain pattern. Suppose, however, you were to sew a piece of fabric that looked just like a current American flag, except that it had 49 stars or 50 six-sided stars (instead of five-sided stars), or white stripes on the very top and very bottom (instead of red), or a blue field that was only six stripes high (instead of seven). Strictly speaking, those pieces of fabric would not be American flags. They would be imperfect approximations of American flags. Would a law against flag burning forbid the desecration of any piece of fabric that even looked like an American flag? What if one takes a big piece of white paper and writes in big boldface letters, "THIS IS AN AMERICAN FLAG," and sets it on fire? Perhaps the courts would rule that any act intended to make onlookers believe that one was burning an American flag would be covered by the amendment. Once again, however, the government would be getting into the business of punishing people for having bad thoughts. This is not the mark of a government in a free society.

What the Flag Means

The flag is a symbol of American values such as self-determination and freedom from oppression. Throughout our history, members of the armed services suffered on behalf of freedom, not on behalf of a piece of fabric. They did not put their lives on the line so that busybodies and bureaucrats could tell us what we can or cannot say and what we can or cannot do with our property.

No doubt, flag burners are often quite vicious, detestable persons whose contempt for American values deserves our contempt. But the law should not forbid all vicious conduct. We can privately refuse to have anything to do with such persons. We can hold them up to public scorn. We might display our patriotism to counter the flag-burning demonstration. Such acts would help solidify the shared citizenship that flag-burning amendment advocates so often invoke. Those informal responses would also help send the message that some matters are best left to private individuals and the free choices they make. Those who take freedom seriously are civilized enough to put flag burners in their place without beating them up or locking them up.

Supporters of laws to punish people who destroy a flag betray their belief that the values the flag symbolizes cannot prevail on their own merits. They seem to think that freedom demands government-mandated respect. But American ideals are sturdy enough to await voluntary respect. Let us repudiate flag burners and persuade (not force) individuals to respect the flag. We must not, however, cheapen the freedoms the flag represents with an amendment that would restrict individual rights.

*"Images of real and virtual child porn . . .
are indistinguishable."*

Virtual Child Pornography
Should Be Banned

Paul M. Rodriguez

In the following viewpoint Paul M. Rodriguez argues that
virtual child pornography—computer-generated depictions
of children engaged in sex acts—is as dangerous to children
as pornography that depicts actual children. He contends
that these pictures are indistinguishable from photographs
and video of real children and may excite predators to molest young children. The government should enact legislation that would outlaw virtual child pornography, in Rodriguez's opinion. In April 2003 Congress passed legislation
that tightened restrictions on real and virtual child pornography and strengthened penalties for repeat offenders. Rodriguez is the managing editor of *Insight on the News*, a biweekly newsmagazine.

As you read, consider the following questions:
1. According to the author, in what important ways is adult
   pornography different from child pornography?
2. Why did pornographers post pictures of normal children
   on their websites, according to Rodriguez?
3. What suggestions does Rodriguez offer to reduce the
   spread of virtual child pornography?

Researching our story about the 2002 Supreme Court decision approving "virtual" child pornography, we wanted to present a visual image that would bring home the horror of this outrage.[1] After extensive calls to the top photo sources failed to produce anything that approximated actual photography of the kind still banned by law, we turned to the Internet. Brother, what a shock it was to see what's out there on the World Wide Web. And we don't mean just every imaginable (or unimaginable) version of hard-core porn, but even the innocent listings that often are attached to pornographic materials.

Equally disturbing (and we'll explain this further on) were porn links that led through images and virtual graphics that seemed not to be pornography at all. In fact, a number of such "binary" sites we found with the help of savvy Webmasters were shocking because they began with the kind of harmless photographs and images of children that might be found in school yearbooks, family albums or Sunday-school bulletins.

The importance of the apparently innocent pictures is, in fact, at the core of our laws against child porn, and it eviscerates the Supreme Court's extraordinarily stupid decision that says virtual images of children used as sexual props is okay because no crime against real children is involved and so publication is protected by the First Amendment.

Endangering Children

Pornography involving consenting adults invokes far different issues than child porn. Our society long ago distinguished the dramatic differences between the two and decided that the latter is aberrant, deviant, depraved and immoral. It endangers the safety of innocent children, which is why it is illegal. It harms children who are exploited foully to make it and it provides a potential catalyst for pederasts and other sexual perverts who may go from images to the real thing—a crime in which victims often are psychologically crippled or even murdered to ensure their silence. So-

---

1. In *Ashcroft v. Free Speech Coalition* in 2002, the Supreme Court decided that the First Amendment protects pornography or other sexual images that only appear to depict real children engaged in sex.

ciety simply decided that the risk of child rape being excited by this stuff is too great to be tolerated.

Indeed, laws against child pornography are designed to accomplish two things: 1) protect children from exploitation for its production and 2) create fire walls to prevent such material from being obtained by wanna-be, in-waiting or impulse-driven child-sex predators who the courts, law enforcement, victims and even the criminals themselves claim are excited to act out their loathsome fantasies by pornographic images of children. The medical profession long has believed that those convicted of child-sex abuse are unlikely ever to be cured of their "illness." Some penologists claim there literally is a 100 percent recidivism rate for pederasts.

Which brings us back to those seemingly innocent photographs and images of children on the Internet. It puzzled us, so we followed an escalating trail of pornographic links with headers such as "virtual porn," "child porn" and similar variations. Not only were the pornographers baiting a virtual path to their hard-core sites with images of innocence, but whoever did this understood that their pederast clientele wants to pursue child sex by sorting through pictures of normal children. The search for the victim is part of the perversion that drives some to harm children.

Unless the government case was completely incompetent, the Supreme Court should have known all of this, yet it ignored the prevention aspects of the law against virtual child porn that it struck down. In doing this the court brazenly and irresponsibly dismissed an essential ingredient of that law: recognition of the effects even virtual child porn has on encouraging potential child molesters.

Indistinguishable from Real Children

In conversations with some of the leading entrepreneurs of virtual technology we learned something else that the apparently ignorant Supreme Court majority overlooked. The industry already can create human images indistinguishable from images of real people and can animate them to do anything at all. Virtual reality is just that—images of computer-generated humans made to act in any way their creators wish them to behave. Check out the image from *Final Fantasy:*

The Spirit Within. . . . The virtual girl appears real in every way. The same thing is being done pornographically, we're told, with virtual children engaging in sexual acts—children indistinguishable from real children to the pederasts, whetting their appetites for molestation.

Feeding the Market

Lack of resources, ever-changing technology, and the free flow of information over the Internet have compounded the already daunting responsibility of law enforcement to eliminate child pornography. Use of computer technology to commit child pornography offenses is at an all-time high. Federal prosecutions of Internet child pornographers have increased by 10 percent every year since 1995, with over 400 cases prosecuted each year in the federal courts alone. Offenders can view and trade child pornography while sitting in the comfort of their homes, an especially attractive option for avoiding detection. Digital technology has enhanced the quality of images available and increased the volume of information that can be accessed. Scanners and inexpensive software packages now allow offenders to create virtual child pornography, which they often trade for more explicit images of real children. The invention of web cameras even allows individuals to molest children in "real time," while others watch from their homes over the Internet. Child pornographers are always seeking more, and more explicit, child pornography. Virtual child pornography feeds this cycle and sustains the market. As technology continues to become cheaper and more advanced, the volume of child pornography being traded over the Internet will rise exponentially.

Daniel S. Armagh, *Cardozo Law Review*, October 20, 2002.

Indeed, we're told by medical and law-enforcement experts, molesters excited by child porn who attack children don't give a damn whether it is real or virtual when the one is indistinguishable from the other. Unfortunately, in its rush to judgment, the liberal majority that now dominates the Supreme Court failed to see the bigger picture. For that matter, it failed even to see the images of real and virtual child porn that are indistinguishable.

Congress and the Bush administration are working to overcome the high court's blunder. Perhaps part of that effort ought to include a cyber-warfare agency that employs the military or intelligence technology now used to hunt down terrorists via the Internet. It should be a relatively simple matter to apply existing child-porn standards against the international child-porn terrorists and their client-agents who are waging a real war against our very real children. Our kids are the ones who are "virtual" targets of child-porn predators.

Thank God we have the First Amendment. It allows us to say directly that the damned-fool Supreme Court justices responsible for this abomination should be horsewhipped.[2]

---

2. In April 2003 Congress passed legislation that narrows the definition of pornography and creates new obscenity offenses to cover virtual and real child pornography that involves visual depictions of prepubescent children and minors. The law also creates a new offense against pandering visual depictions as child pornography and strengthens penalties for repeat offenders.

"Virtual-porn prohibitions are especially easy to abuse."

Virtual Child Pornography Should Not Be Banned

Wendy Kaminer

According to Wendy Kaminer in the following viewpoint, virtual child pornography is protected speech because real children are not harmed in its production. The images depicted in virtual pornography are computer-generated, so real children are not forced to have sex, she argues. Moreover, Kaminer maintains that there is no evidence to suggest that virtual child pornography incites pedophiles to molest children. In April 2003 Congress passed legislation that tightened restrictions on real and virtual child pornography and strengthened penalties for repeat offenders. Kaminer is a senior correspondent for the *American Prospect* and a contributing editor at the *Atlantic Monthly*. She also serves on the national board of the American Civil Liberties Union.

As you read, consider the following questions:
1. As reported by Kaminer, what does the Child Pornography Prevention Act (CPPA) of 1996 prohibit?
2. According to Kaminer, why do defenders of CPPA equate virtual with actual pornography?
3. Why does the ban on virtual child pornography depend on the subjective reaction of viewers?

It is possible, of course, that computer-simulated images of virtual children having virtual sex may encourage pedophiles to act on their impulses or may assist them in seducing children. There is, however, little or no empirical evidence that these images have such dire effects. Congress criminalized virtual child porn anyway.

The Child Pornography Prevention Act of 1996 (CPPA) prohibits computer images that "appear" to show actual children engaged in sex; it also bans advertising, promoting, or describing any sexually explicit images "in such a manner that conveys the impression" that actual children are depicted. Antiporn activists insist that this ban on virtual porn is essential to protecting children and enforcing laws against actual child pornography, since prosecutors may not be able to distinguish the actual from the virtual variety. Free-speech advocates charge that the CPPA allows for the prosecution of thought crimes, by criminalizing non-obscene renderings of imaginary children engaged in imaginary sex. The federal courts are divided on the constitutionality of this statute: It was struck down by the Ninth Circuit Court of Appeals and upheld by the First, Fourth, and 11th Circuit Courts. The issue is now before the Supreme Court.[1]

Many civil libertarians have long accepted (and supported) bans on depicting actual children engaged in actual sex. Traditional child-porn laws need not rely on speculation about the harm caused by the distribution of sexually explicit images involving minors; they can rely instead on the harm caused by the *production* of sexually explicit images involving minors.

But laws against depictions of imaginary children can rely only on imaginary evidence of harm. As the Ninth Circuit . . . observed in *Free Speech Coalition v. Reno*: "Factual studies that establish the link between computer-generated child pornography and the subsequent sexual abuse of children apparently do not yet exist."[2] Indeed, in enacting the CPPA, Congress relied on the report of the pornography commission led by former Attorney General Edwin Meese in the

1. In *Ashcroft v. Free Speech Coalition* in 2002, the Supreme Court decided that the First Amendment protects pornography or other sexual images that only appear to depict real children engaged in sex.   2. In 2001 the case was called *Free Speech Coalition v. Reno*; in 2002 the case became *Ashcroft v. Free Speech Coalition*.

1980s, a study that addressed only the suspected harms of pornography involving actual children. In other words, the Ninth Circuit stressed, the CPPA relies on findings that "predate" the technology it targets.

An Indirect Link

Virtual child pornography is not "intrinsically related" to the sexual abuse of children. While the Government asserts that the images can lead to actual instances of child abuse, the causal link is contingent and indirect. The harm does not necessarily follow from the speech, but depends upon some unquantified potential for subsequent criminal acts.

Anthony M. Kennedy, *Ashcroft v. Free Speech Coalition*, 2002.

Still, defenders of the CPPA equate actual and virtual porn, simply because they are difficult to distinguish visually. "Both actual and counterfeit child pornography will pass for the real thing and incite pedophiles to molest and children to be victims," according to a brief filed by the National Law Center for Children and Families and several other conservative advocacy groups. "If the pedophile and the child victim cannot tell the difference, there is no difference in the effect conveyed." What's wrong with this reasoning? (Put aside the callous disregard of the difference to real children who are forced to have sex in the production of real pornography.) It assumes its conclusion—that virtual child porn incites pedophilia and creates "child victims"—and it advocates criminalizing speech because of its presumed effect on a particular class of listeners: people inclined toward child abuse.

Courts confront this argument repeatedly in First Amendment cases, particularly in cases involving pornography. In 1985, in *American Booksellers Association v. Hudnut*, the Seventh Circuit Court of Appeals struck down a local antiporn ordinance that was based on the assumption that pornography leads to the objectification of women and contributes to sexual violence and discrimination. Accepting this assumption for the sake of argument, the appeals court pointed out its inadequacies: "All of these unhappy effects depend on mental intermediation." In others words, the power of speech is collaborative.

Since the ban on virtual child porn relies heavily on the subjective reactions of viewers, speakers are given little notice of precisely what speech is criminalized. When Congress bans sexually explicit material that "appears" to depict minors engaged in sex, you have to ask, "Appears to whom?" A lot of people over 40 have trouble distinguishing 19-year-olds from precocious 15-year-olds. The CPPA could easily be construed to prohibit non-obscene sexually explicit images of young adults. The statute does provide its targets with a defense: that the alleged child porn in fact involved an actual person, who was an adult at the time the image was produced (so this defense does not apply in cases of virtual child porn) and the image was not promoted in a way that "conveyed the impression" that it involved a minor. "Conveyed to whom?" you have to ask.

What are people talking about when they talk about child porn? That depends. Some point to Calvin Klein ads or the movie adaptations of *Lolita* (not to mention the book). *The Tin Drum*, a 1979 film based on a novel by Gunter Grass, is considered pornographic in Oklahoma City: A few years ago, local officials confiscated copies of this allegedly dangerous film, which includes a scene suggestive of oral sex between a six-year-old boy and a teenage girl. A court in Oklahoma judged the film obscene.

Some supporters of CPPA will dismiss cases like this as "horror stories," suggesting that they're rare or even apocryphal. In fact, they're fairly common, as anyone familiar with the history of censorship knows. Virtual-porn prohibitions are especially easy to abuse, since evidence of social, scientific, or artistic value is irrelevant to a charge of child pornography. (Speech must be found to have no redeeming value to be considered obscene.) How will the CPPA be applied by a Justice Department led by right-wingers? Senator Jesse Helms includes some sex-education materials in his definition of child porn.[3] Soon speech may be no safer than sex.

3. In April 2003 Congress passed legislation that narrows the definition of pornography and creates new obscenity offenses to cover virtual and real child pornography that involves visual depictions of prepubescent children and minors. The law also creates a new offense against pandering visual depictions as child pornography and strengthens penalties for repeat offenders.

Periodical Bibliography

The following articles have been selected to supplement the diverse views presented in this chapter.

Anonymous	"The Assault on Civil Liberties," *Progressive*, August 2000.
Russell Blackford	"Free Speech and Hate Speech," *Quadrant*, January 2001.
Robert Bork	"The Sanctity of Smut," *Wall Street Journal*, April 23, 2002.
Jonah Goldberg	"Free Speech Rots from the Inside Out," *American Enterprise*, January/February 2003.
Marjorie Heins	"Screening Out Sex: Kids, Computers, and the New Censors," *American Prospect*, July 1, 1998.
Daniel Hellinger	"Taking Liberties with the Constitution," *Synthesis/Regeneration*, Spring 2002.
Nat Hentoff	"How Free Is Free Speech?" *World & I*, April 2001.
James Huff	"Filtering Behavior Instead of Speech," *American Libraries*, April 1999.
Wendy Kaminer	"Bigots' Rights," *American Prospect*, June 19, 2000.
Wendy Kaminer	"Virtual Offensiveness," *American Prospect*, November 19, 2001.
Stanley Kurtz	"Free Speech and an Orthodoxy of Dissent," *Chronicle of Higher Education*, October 26, 2001.
Joshua Micah Marshall	"Will Free Speech Get Tangled in the Net?" *American Prospect*, January/February 1998.
Alex Torralbas	"How the Net Endangers a Basic American Liberty," *Computerworld*, April 3, 2000.

CHAPTER 2

Should Church and State Be Separate?

Chapter Preface

The public school system has long been a focal point in the battle over the separation of church and state. The most recent dispute, over whether tax dollars should be used to fund private—often religious—school tuition highlights the tension between those who advocate strict separation between church and state and people who support some merging of religion and government.

School vouchers, also known as scholarships, redirect the flow of education funding, channeling it directly to individual families rather than to school districts. In effect the state returns money collected from parents in the form of taxes for the public school system to families in order to help them finance their child's education in the public or private school of their choice. Supporters of school vouchers argue that the program will foster competition among public and private schools and improve education for all children. In addition, they argue that the program does not violate the principle of separation of church and state because school vouchers can be used for religious or secular schools.

Opponents of school vouchers contend that because parents can use taxpayer money to send their children to parochial schools, vouchers infringe on the doctrine of separation of church and state. In support of their opposition, many people cite a 1971 Supreme Court decision, *Lemon v. Kurtzman*, which laid out the so-called "Lemon test" to determine whether a statute violated the policy of separation of church and state. Under *Lemon*, any statute must have a secular purpose, the primary effect of the statute must be one that neither advances nor inhibits religion, and the statute must not foster excessive government entanglement with religion. Because one of the primary goals of sectarian schools is to teach religion, voucher opponents argue that using tax funds for religious school tuition fails the Lemon test. As stated in a brief filed against a school voucher program in Wisconsin, "By offering publicly funded sectarian private education as the principle alternative to public schooling, [school vouchers] can be regarded as advancing religion and creating a symbolic union between church and state."

Despite widespread opposition, school voucher advocates secured a landmark victory in 2002 when the Supreme Court decided that a voucher program in Cleveland, Ohio, did not violate the doctrine of separation of church and state. The ruling reverses an appeals court decision, which struck down the program in 2000 because nearly all the families receiving the tax-supported state tuition scholarships sent their children to Catholic schools in Cleveland. According to Chief Justice William Rehnquist, "We believe the program challenged here is a program of true private choice. The Ohio program is neutral in all respects toward religion. It is part of a general and multifaceted undertaking by the state of Ohio to provide educational opportunities to the children of a failed school district."

Despite the victory in Cleveland, most state-elected school voucher programs have been found unconstitutional by the courts, including programs in Florida, Vermont, Maine, and Pennsylvania. Other states—including California, Colorado, and Washington—have voted against implementing school voucher programs. Whether school vouchers will become more widespread remains to be seen. For now, the debate over school vouchers reflects the division of opinion over to what extent church and state should be separate. The authors in the following chapter debate other issues surrounding the doctrine of separation of church and state.

"The best way to avoid favoring one religion over another may be to treat them all in a hands-off manner."

Church and State Should Be Separate

Alan Wolfe

In the following viewpoint Alan Wolfe examines Philip Hamburger's position, outlined in his book *Separation of Church and State*, that the framers of the Constitution did not intend strict separation of church and state. Wolfe contends that the Constitution was written to accommodate changing ideals and values—just because the framers may not have thought it critical to include a requirement that church and state be separate does not mean that instituting separation today would be unconstitutional. Moreover, according to Wolfe, blending religion with politics increases the risk of corruption within government. He notes that all too often governments dominated by members of majority religions make policies that harm members of minority faiths. Thus, Wolfe argues, church and state are best kept separate. Wolfe is the director of the Boisi Center for Religion and American Public Life at Boston College and the author of *Moral Freedom: The Search for Virtue in a World of Choice.*

As you read, consider the following questions:

1. According to Wolfe, what did Thomas Jefferson state in his famous letter to the Danbury Baptists?
2. According to Philip Hamburger, when did the secular ideal of separation of church and state emerge?

Alan Wolfe, "Why Separation of Church and State Is Still a Good Idea," *Books & Culture*, September/October 2002. Copyright © 2002 by Alan Wolfe. Reproduced by permission.

In 1947, the U.S. Supreme Court decided the case of *Everson v. Board of Education* and thereby officially enshrined into American constitutional law the principle of separation of church and state. New Jersey had passed a law providing state-subsidized busing to all students, those who attended parochial schools as well as those who attended public ones. In his opinion for the majority, Justice [Hugo] Black invoked the metaphor of a "wall" of separation (used once or twice in earlier Court decisions) that Thomas Jefferson had coined in his letter to the Danbury Baptists, written in 1802. All of our contemporary debates over separation—whether they involve crèches [Nativity scenes] in public places or the [2002] effort by the Ninth Circuit Court to remove the words "under God" from the Pledge of Allegiance—trace themselves back to *Everson*.

Immediately after the *Everson* decision, the *Washington Post* editorialized that "the principle at issue is one of the most fundamental in the American concept of government—the separation of church and state." Philip Hamburger's book [*Separation of Church and State*] is dedicated to proving that just about every word in that editorial's sentence is incorrect.

Historical Precedent

Far from having roots in the American past, almost none of our early writers and politicians, Hamburger shows, accepted the notion of separation of church and state. When the term was used at all, it meant simply that politics and religion were different kinds of activities, not that the one should be kept entirely out of the other. Early theorists generally held that a good society *required* religion and its attendant morality, so that, when they used the term *separation of church and state*, they were not defending an ideal but launching an attack on those who *denied* such a self-evident truth. Nor did dissenting religions dissent from this consensus, for even if they believed in the principle, which not all of them did, they generally kept silent about it, given how unpopular the principle was.

To illustrate these points, Hamburger goes right to the heart of the matter—Jefferson's famous letter. It turns out that the Danbury Baptists were not all that happy with Jefferson's advice; they never published Jefferson's letter to them. Like other Baptists then (and to some degree now), their objections were to an establishment that, in linking itself to the political world, lost its purity of faith. Religion, as the Connecticut Baptists put it in 1803, should be "distinct" from the state because rights of conscience were given by God, not by men. This is not Jefferson's deism. It is rather an attempt to preserve religion's special mission against worldly corruption.

Separation of church and state, as Hamburger tells the story, did finally come to America during the 19th century. But it did not come as the triumph of reason; it was instead the product of Protestant nativism seeking to wage war against Catholicism. "Our sole object is to form a barrier high and eternal as the Andes, which shall forever separate the Church from the State," wrote the American Republican Party of New York in 1845.

In the very next paragraph of its declaration, however, the party went on to say that "we believe the Holy Bible, without sectarian note or comment, to be a most proper and necessary book, as well for our children as ourselves, and we are determined that they shall not be deprived of it, either in, or out of school." Implicit in this passage is that a wall should be established between government and sects rather than between government and faith. And Protestants, as they understood themselves, were not sectarian; they believed that they acted as individuals, not as corporate entities. Their entreaties about keeping government and religion distinct applied only to Catholics, not to themselves. Indeed some Protestant denominations like the Presbyterians, which had at earlier times been accused of authoritarianism, could turn around and charge Catholics with the same crime, thereby absolving themselves.

Only in the late 19th and early 20th century, according to Hamburger, can we begin to see the emergence of a secular ideal of separation of church and state. And even when it did come, the modern conception of separationism was not as enlightened as it claimed. For one thing, a surprising amount of anti-Catholicism persisted into the 20th century;

Paul Blanshard's book *American Freedom and Catholic Power*, a liberal attack on the Church, appeared as late as 1948, the year after *Everson*. And liberals who urged separation between church and state had their own distinctive form of religious faith. They could be as censorious and intolerant as the most fanatical believers. They tried to substitute secular rituals for religious ones. They held fast to transcendental ideals of national purpose. "While hostile to Christianity and any other distinct religion," Hamburger writes, "the Liberals glowed with religious intensity."

All these strands came together in the *Everson* case. Arch Everson, who brought the suit, was a member of an organization, the Junior Order of United American Mechanics, that had its origins in 19th-century nativism; his lawyer, Albert McCay, had represented similar groups in earlier cases. More important, the author of the Court's majority decision, Hugo Black, had been a member of the Ku Klux Klan, the most notorious anti-Catholic organization in American history. Hence Black's invoking the ideal of separation of church and state serves to remind Hamburger of the more unsavory history of this particular doctrine. And it thus throws into question decisions by the Court since *Everson* that rely on the doctrine of separation of church and state to keep religion out of American public life.

Undermining His Case

Hamburger has written an extremely important book. His prodigious learning and ingenious interpretations overturn the conventional wisdom, forcing even the most passionate defenders of separationism to recognize how much of the story of religious liberty has taken on mythical dimensions. Still, the book is written more as legal brief than as a work of historical scholarship. Hamburger has a point of view to push, and he pushes so intently that he sometimes undermines his own case.

If Hugo Black were really trying to impose on the country views he once held as a nativist, surely he should have declared public support for Catholic busing unconstitutional. Yet he did the exact opposite in *Everson;* as judges often do, he announced a principle that he did not apply to the case at hand. Hamburger claims that Black nonetheless "understood what he was doing." In this interpretation, Black was trying to sneak into law a conception of separation even while appeasing Catholics by allowing them to think they won the specific case. But jurisprudence since *Everson* suggests that Black did not know what he was doing, as Hamburger himself seems to acknowledge by citing Black's contention that he had won only a Pyrrhic victory. The Supreme Court has waffled back and forth on the question of separationism ever since, never able to set firm guidelines. Black's real legacy is that he left everyone confused, not that he had a predetermined plan.

Branch. © 1995 by *San Antonio Express News*. Reprinted with permission.

One reason Black waffled, furthermore, was that he had changed his views considerably since the days he joined the Klan. There is much about Black not to like, even, if not especially, in his most liberal phase; he could be arrogant and brittle in his views. But it is extremely unfair of Hamburger to see the stain of Black's Klan membership behind his decisions as a judge. Black may indeed have had a lifelong suspicion of Catholics—Hamburger quotes an interesting observation by Black's son on that point—but *Everson*, because it in fact upheld the busing, can just as easily be interpreted as a way for Black to reach out to Catholics for his past sins, an estimable, rather than a despicable, thing to do.

Insincere Separationists

Hamburger's one-sided interpretation of Black's role in *Everson* is characteristic of much of his book. Although he never comes right out and accuses advocates of separationism of hypocrisy, he consistently implies that they were insincere. At one point he notes that liberals were opportunistic; having long argued that America required a constitutional amendment to establish the principle of separationism, they turned around and began to argue that separation was an idea already inscribed in the Constitution itself. And by showing that while liberals were hostile to religion, they clearly had religious longings of their own. Hamburger believes he's demonstrated once and for all that their strict arguments on behalf of separationism should not be taken at face value, since they had no inclination to separate government from their favored religious dispensations.

But neither of these points is convincing. The history of American jurisprudence is filled with examples of lawyers seeking to build the strongest possible cases for their clients or causes, dropping one argument and employing another if it promises a greater chance of success, even if it seems to contradict the first. Many of the groups whose history Hamburger recounts, and not just the separationists, were divided in their opinions or changed their minds, including the Baptists.

Nor is it hypocritical to argue for separation of church and state and at the same time to hold views that are semi-religious. If anything, the implied hypocrisy here is something we ought to welcome. At the end of the film version of *Inherit the Wind*, Spencer Tracy, who plays the Clarence Darrow figure, having attacked religion throughout the film, begins to speak in quasi-religious terms and is immediately attacked as a hypocrite by Gene Kelley, the H.L. Mencken figure.[1] But it is Tracy who is the more sympathetic character. Surely we should want our anti-clericalists

1. *Inherit the Wind* is a film based on the real-life trial in 1925 of teacher John T. Scopes, who was accused of the crime of teaching evolution instead of creationism.

to have a touch of belief about them, especially when compared to the truly cynical.

Reasons to Believe

Ultimately, Hamburger offers no credible reasons why anyone would genuinely believe in the separation of church and state in the first place. But there *are* good reasons to believe in the principle. Religion has been used to coerce members of minority faiths in this country. Opportunities for corruption are presented whenever government and religion work too closely together. In an era of religious diversity such as our own, the best way to avoid favoring one religion over another may be to treat them all in a hands-off manner.

Yet so intent is Hamburger on finding examples of bad faith, he tends to ignore many of the principled concerns of Jewish writers who worried about the integrity of their faith in a predominantly Christian America and of Catholic thinkers like John Courtney Murray, who worked strenuously to change the views of his church toward greater sympathy for the principle of church-state separation.

Jefferson's letter to the Danbury Baptists, Hamburger concludes, is little more than a "fig leaf." And once it is removed, we will no longer need to be in thrall to strict constructions of separationism. "In discussion of these and other issues," he writes, "separation ought not be assumed to have any special legitimacy as an early American and thus constitutional idea." In this, he is no doubt correct; his account of the history is convincing. But then he goes on to conclude that "precisely because of its history—both its lack of constitutional authority and its development in response to prejudice—the idea of separation should, at best, be viewed with suspicion." In this, by contrast, I believe he is wrong.

The Constitution, as Hamburger notes, is a living document. Because it is, many of our most cherished contemporary ideals had no special constitutional authority in the eighteenth century: freedom of speech as we currently understand it is one; racial equality is another. When we evaluate a contemporary constitutional principle, we need to ask two important questions. The first is whether there is a basis for the idea in early American life and in the Constitution. The second is whether it is a good idea. It is clear from Hamburger's own account that earlier generations of America believed in notions out of which our current conception of separation could rightly grow, such as the notion that politics and faith are distinct realms of life. Just because the idea was not endorsed in the 18th century the way it has been interpreted in the 20th does not make it alien to our history and traditions. Contemporary scholars may exaggerate the importance of Jefferson's 1802 letter, but the important question, which Hamburger never addresses, is why that letter became so important to our current conceptions.

Nothing in the history of a doctrine, furthermore, answers the question of whether the doctrine makes sense. Different people will have different answers to the question of whether separation is a good idea, which is only proper in a constitutional democracy. But Hamburger seems to want to cut that debate off, even charging that his ideological opponents— the strict separationists—treat those who disagree with them as "un-American." A debate will and should take place no matter how tortured the path of the doctrine's evolution.

Surprisingly, perhaps, given the thrust of his argument, Hamburger never says explicitly that he wants separation of church and state abandoned. Nor does he propose an alternative, other than to note that there are other possible paths besides pure union of church and state on the one hand and pure separation on the other. His book, therefore, for all its strengths, ends limply, cautioning us against the metaphor of the wall without addressing in concrete terms specific cases and how they might better be decided.

Until another doctrine comes along to replace Jefferson's metaphor, separation of church and state is here to stay. But even though it is unlikely to be thrown out any time soon, separationism will clearly be moderated, as evidenced by the June 2002 decision allowing school vouchers, a contemporary replay of the *Everson* case.[2] That kind of slow transformation, and not Hamburger's sometimes more apocalyptic musings, is the appropriate approach to this extremely important issue.

2. In 2002 the Supreme Court decided that public money could be used to underwrite tuition at religious schools as long as parents have a choice among a range of religious and secular schools.

"*The Founders [of the United States] had no intention of banishing Christianity in general from the halls of government.*"

Church and State Should Not Be Separate

Steve Bonta

According to Steve Bonta in the following viewpoint, the Declaration of Independence states that God is the source of all rights, including "life, liberty, and the pursuit of happiness." Government, he argues, exists merely to protect the rights that God has bestowed upon humanity. In Bonta's opinion, when church and state are separated, citizens are no longer ruled by God's moral codes but by tyrannical governments. Bonta is a contributing editor for the *New American*, a conservative, biweekly journal.

As you read, consider the following questions:
1. According to the author, why does a government under God depend on its citizens' moral and religious conduct?
2. Which historical event originated the first statement that rights were conferred by a government instead of God, as reported by Bonta?
3. In Bonta's opinion, what desire has driven most of man's progress throughout history?

Steve Bonta, "One Nation Under God: The Supremacy of God as Creator, Lawgiver, and Source of Individual Rights Is at the Center of Our Nation's Vision of Liberty Under Law," *New American*, vol. 18, July 9, 2002, p. 10.

If ever there were a first principle of political thought, a bedrock premise on which all other political, legal, and social reasoning should be founded, it is that God is the Source of all rights. As with the physical creation, so with the spiritual and the moral: God is the final cause and origin of all things pertaining to man. As the Declaration of Independence states so emphatically, He endows men with "certain unalienable Rights," among which are "Life, Liberty, and the Pursuit of Happiness."

The consequences of this single, ultimate fact, that rights come from God and not from any earthly source, are far-reaching. The great French political theorist Frederic Bastiat pointed out in *The Law* that "each of us has a natural right—from God—to defend his person, his liberty, and his property." From this individual right of self-defense, Bastiat then derived collective rights, observing that "it follows that a group of men have the right to organize and support a common force to protect these rights constantly. Thus the principle of collective right—its reason for existing, its lawfulness—is based on individual right." Therefore, if we assume that God bestows rights on individuals, we must also acknowledge that the individual is superior to the collective, and therefore to the State—the "common force" Bastiat spoke of.

As Bastiat indicates, government—the "common force"—exists to protect only that which the people have legitimately received from the Almighty: their God-given rights. In the words of the Declaration, "to secure these Rights, Governments are instituted among Men, deriving their just Powers from the Consent of the Governed." For example, since God has given to man the right to acquire and to control property "by the sweat of his brow," it follows that properly constituted government must protect that right. But it should not empower man to wrest property from his neighbor, since God has never authorized men to steal from one another. Likewise, government must protect the individual's right to defend himself, but it may not, without violating the laws of God, commit murder or authorize its citizens to do so. And certainly no legitimate government can prohibit a man from praying or from invoking the name of Deity; of all the privileges vouchsafed by God to his children, the privilege of supplicating the Almighty, for aid, for strength, for pardon, or for any other purpose, is surely the most important. Any government placing barriers between man and God by forbidding him to pray in public places is no better than Nebuchadnezzar's Babylon, which prohibited worshipping the God of Israel and required men instead to bow down to the golden idol of the State.

The Trouble with Separation

So obsessed are separationists with the supposedly baleful influence of religion on democracy that they ignore the many ways, some good (and some perhaps questionable), that democracy influences religion. As long ago as the beginning of the 19th century, [French politician and writer Alexis de] Tocqueville noted that unlike in Europe, religion in America was already substantially democratized. Although the process has worked mostly by osmosis, sometimes the government has stepped in directly, as in the 1878 case in which the Supreme Court ruled against a Mormon who defended his right to practice polygamy on religious grounds. The trouble with strict separation, in other words, is not only that it deprives the state of the sustenance it gains from religion, but that it also spares religion from the moderating influence of liberal and republican principles.

Adam Wolfson, *Commentary*, October 2002.

Another consequence of the doctrine that God is the author of rights is that individuals are primarily amenable to God, not the State, for their conduct. In the words of James Madison, "before any man can be considered as a member of Civil Society, he must be considered as a subject of the Governour of the Universe." For this reason, limited republican government under God depends crucially on its citizenry's moral and religious conduct. George Washington observed, in his Farewell Address, that "of all the dispositions and habits which lead to political prosperity, religion and morality are indispensable supports." Samuel Adams warned that "neither the wisest constitution nor the wisest laws will secure the liberty and happiness of a people whose manners are universally corrupt." And John Adams stressed that "our Constitution was made only for a moral and religious people. It is wholly inadequate to the government of any other." It is simply impossible to imagine a limited, enduring republic without God and without morality, since, as English statesman Edmund Burke, a contemporary of the Founders, so trenchantly observed, "society cannot exist unless a controlling power upon the will and appetite be placed somewhere, and the less of it there is within, the more there must be without. It is ordained in the eternal constitution of things, that men of intemperate minds cannot be free. Their passions forge their fetters."

Republican governments under God, then, are the truest champions of liberty. God, the source of all of man's attributes, obviously has created us with varied and unequal endowments of talents. Under conditions of liberty, men and women of equal God-given rights deploy their diverse and unequal God-given skills to create a society where every individual benefits from the talents of others.

Government Without God

When God is removed from the calculus of government, all of these attributes of God-given liberty are turned on their heads. It was the French Revolution, that grotesque parody of the American founding, which first enshrined the heresy that rights are transmitted to the individual, not by God, but by the Almighty Collective or "general will." According to the French Declaration of the Rights of Man and Citizen, the counterfeit of our glorious Declaration of Independence, all sovereignty (i.e., power) resides "essentially in the nation. No group, no individual may exercise authority not emanating expressly therefrom." The French sansculottes, in substituting for God the will of the majority, completely inverted the relationship of individual to state. Government, which they believed to have originated by majoritarian consent, conferred rights on individuals, reserving to itself the power to revise or retract them any time it chose.

From this distorted premise flow distorted ideas, which have been responsible for much of man's suffering at the hands of the State. For if there is no God, then the State must reign supreme, and all must obey its edicts. Morality then becomes mere obedience to man-made, positive law, and subject to change at the whims of rulers. Instead of equality under the law, egalitarianism—the radical urge to suppress and level individual achievement—becomes the order of the day. Among the clamoring interest groups that replace individuals as the fundamental political units, strength depends on conformity to mass standards rather than on independent thought and action. Moreover, since individuals are no longer the crucial building blocks on which government depends, personal virtue and self-discipline are no longer needed. Such government does not have liberty as its goal, but seeks instead to exercise raw force. It must therefore be freed from all moral, legal, and religious restraints to achieve its full destructive potential.

These two great polarities are completely irreconcilable. Either men will serve God, and frame government to protect God-given rights, thereby maximizing human liberty, or they will serve the exalted State, the most powerful agency man can create when left to his own devices. Only a State acknowledging God as an authority superior to itself will resist the tidal pull of tyranny.

Church and State

But then what of the Founders' insistence, in the First Amendment to the U.S. Constitution, on Congress making "no law respecting an establishment of religion, or prohibiting the free exercise thereof"? Doesn't this mean that a "wall of separation between church and state," in Jefferson's famous phrase, should be erected at every level of government?

First, there is an important distinction between a "church" or an "established religion," on one hand, and "religion" in general on the other. The phrase "established religion" referred in the Founders' day to an official or state religion such as the Church of England. Both the Founders and the English jurist William Blackstone, whose writings on English law were widely read by the Founders, often used such terminology. Blackstone, in his *Commentaries on the Laws of England*, wrote of England's established church:

> If . . . men quarrel with the ecclesiastical establishment, the civil magistrate has nothing to do with it. . . . [But the civil magistrate] is bound to protect the established church. . . . For, if every sect were to be indulged in a free communion of

civil employments, the idea of a national establishment would at once be destroyed, and the episcopal church would no longer be the church of England.

The First Amendment, then, prohibits not the public exercise of faith but the establishment by law of a particular sect as the official national religion. The Founders had no intention of banishing Christianity in general from the halls of government; they saw their country and the government they had founded as essentially Christian. According to Joseph Story, a Supreme Court justice appointed by President [James] Monroe and arguably the foremost legal and constitutional scholar of his generation:

> [A]t the time of the adoption of the Constitution, and of the [First Amendment], the general, if not the universal sentiment was, that Christianity ought to receive encouragement from the state, so far as was not incompatible with the private rights of conscience and the freedom of religious worship. An attempt to level all religions, and to make it a matter of state policy to hold all in utter indifference, would have created universal disapprobation, if not universal indignation.

Protecting Religion from the Government

Contrary to what many assume, the First Amendment's "establishment clause" was intended to protect religion from the government, and not the reverse. As Madison put it, "because Religion be exempt from the authority of the Society at large, still less can it be subject to that of the Legislative Body. The latter are but creatures and viceregents of the former. . . . The preservation of a free Government requires not merely, that the metes and bounds which separate each department of power be invariably maintained; but more especially that neither of them be suffered to overleap the great Barrier which defends the rights of the people."

The Founders intended the "establishment clause," like the rest of the First Amendment and much of the rest of the Bill of Rights, to apply only to the federal and not to state governments. For this reason, the Founders used the words "Congress shall make no law. . . ." (Several state governments at the time of the Founding did in fact have "established" churches.) While many of the Founders might have disagreed in principle with this circumstance, they believed that the overarching principle of federalism—of limiting the federal government to certain constitutionally enumerated powers and leaving the rest up to the states and to the people—was more important still. Almost a century after the founding, the 44th Congress in 1876 considered adding a constitutional amendment that would prohibit the states from having any "established religion." However, even in the turbulent post–Civil War period, when many Americans had come to view states' rights as hostile to the Lincolnian dogma of union at any cost, most members of Congress still understood the principle of federalism relative to religion. New York's Senator [Francis] Kernan, citing the proposed amendment, said:

> "No State shall make any law respecting an establishment of religion, or prohibiting the free exercise thereof; and no religious test shall ever be required as a qualification to any office or public trust under any State." That provision has my most hearty commendation; but for all that it is not necessary to put it in the Federal Constitution. That matter was discussed in the convention that made the Constitution, and it was not thought wise to put in any such provision, but to leave it to the States. . . . There is a provision in the constitution of [New Hampshire] that no one can be elected governor unless he is of the Protestant religion, and so as to members of the Legislature of the State. But I am willing to trust that to the people of that State, believing that very soon in this age of ours and in this country of ours they will adopt the liberal provisions which are found in the constitutions of the other States on the subject of the sacred rights of conscience.

Senator [Lewis] Bogy of Missouri, during the same period, observed:

> And among the most sacred of these rights, lying at the very foundation of all liberty, was that of freedom of conscience and the right to worship God according to the dictates of each one's individual conviction. That was left to the States, and was not placed . . . under the control of the Federal Government. The attempt here to exercise this power takes from the States that right and gives it to the Federal Government.

For over a hundred years after America's founding, no one questioned the intent of the "establishment clause" nor the notion that, while America recognized no official religion, the United States and her form of government were fundamentally Christian, enshrining Christian values in her legal code and recognizing the Judeo-Christian God as the supreme authority over the affairs of men.

Secularizing the State

Unfortunately, with the advance of militant secularism in the 20th century, the government in general and the Supreme Court in particular began looking for ways to exclude religion from the public domain altogether. They began using as the flimsiest of pretexts for their attacks on religion both the First Amendment and the Fourteenth Amendment—the latter having been passed after the Civil War, to guarantee that no state could "deprive any person of life, liberty, or property, without due process of law; nor deny to any person within its jurisdiction the equal protection of the laws." The Fourteenth Amendment was intended to protect citizens' rights to due process—that is, the "right to be tried by independent and unprejudiced courts using established procedures and applying valid pre-existing laws," as former Supreme Court Justice Hugo Black defined the term. It also required the states to give all persons equal protection under the laws. Neither of these passages are remotely connected with the establishment of state religion, but by 1940, the Supreme Court could assert, in *Cantwell v. Connecticut*, that "the fundamental concept of liberty embodied in the Fourteenth Amendment embraces the liberties guaranteed by the First Amendment. The First Amendment declares that Congress shall make no law respecting an establishment of religion or prohibiting the exercise thereof. The Fourteenth Amendment has rendered the legislatures of the states as incompetent as Congress to enact such laws." Supreme Court Justice Felix Frankfurter blithely claimed in 1948 that "we are all agreed that the First and the Fourteenth Amendments have a secular reach far more penetrating in the conduct of Government than merely to forbid an 'established church.'"

Following such pronouncements, the floodgates opened. In 1962, the Supreme Court, in *Engel v. Vitale*, inexplicably discovered a constitutional prohibition on prayer in public schools. From that day to this, America has been barraged with court decisions similar in tone to Engel, effectively exiling Christian culture, morality, and symbolism from public life. We've seen court decrees banning prayer at school athletic events, mandating the removal of creches [Nativity scenes] and Christmas decorations from government property, and ordering displays of the Ten Commandments in courtrooms to be taken down. At the same time, the courts have protected the alleged rights of the vilest of pornographers, abortionists, and political subversives to ply their nefarious trades. In effect, the government is not driving religion per se out of government, but merely replacing Judeo-Christian values with the humanistic doctrine of exalted, amoral Man.

So-called modern man fancies himself unique in his secular, humanistic worldview, but in truth he is merely an ugly historical anomaly. Throughout most of human history, progress has been driven primarily by religion, by man's desire to glorify the Almighty. All of the advances in limited government that prepared the way for the American founding came about as men in the various European nations groped for ways to configure government so as to please God and to agree with the God-given constraints of natural law. The mightiest works of art and architecture, from the towering Gothic cathedrals of the high Middle Ages to the soaring music of Bach and Handel, were all the products of men seeking to glorify God by fulfilling the highest human impulses. The same could be said of most of the greatest inventors and scientists, at least until fairly recently. There are few historical precedents of a people so obsessed with themselves that they permit their government to decapitate their culture by removing religion from all but the most private domains. . . .

America, however, cannot deny God's supremacy and remain free. To drift away from our Christian moorings is to chart a course into bondage, both spiritual and political. The French Revolutionaries and others of their ilk began by erecting secular, even anti-Christian states glorifying Man, and ended up enslaving themselves under mob rule, guided and harnessed by tyrants and demagogues. For us there can be no middle ground; we either mimic the mistakes of those who turned their backs on their Creator, or keep both ourselves and our government subservient to the supreme Law-giver, remaining, as our Founders hoped, one nation under God.

> *"Removing federal discrimination against faith-based providers of social services will provide more avenues of help for the needy."*

Faith-Based Charitable Organizations Should Receive Federal Funds

Tony Hall

In the following viewpoint Tony Hall argues in favor of a bill that would allow faith-based charitable organizations to receive federal funding. He contends that the bill would allow all organizations—secular or religious—that perform social services to compete on a level playing field for public funds. Religious organizations provide beneficial services to society and thus should be eligible to receive government funding, he maintains. Hall is the democratic representative of Ohio and the founder and chairman of the Congressional Hunger Center. As of this writing, the Community Solutions Act had been passed by the House and was being debated in the Senate.

As you read, consider the following questions:
1. According to the author, what is the intent of expanding federal funding to religious organizations?
2. As noted by Hall, what does the Community Solutions Act not do?
3. How would the bill encourage charitable giving, as explained by Hall?

The Community Solutions Act (H.R. 7) aims to help a broad range of organizations that are assisting Americans in need.[1] Speaker of the House Dennis Hastert (R-Illinois) and fellow Congressman J.C. Watts (R-Oklahoma) are great allies in this effort, and I am very glad to join them in launching it.

I have seen many frontline organizations at work, and I believe this bill will help them bring their energy and creativity to bear on our social problems, just as small businesses have invigorated our economy. The problems these groups tackle affect a significant number of people; for example, hunger plagues more than 1 in 10 Americans.

People in need are more than just clients of social outreach programs; they are also my own constituents, and they deserve more attention from Congress—and more places to turn when they seek help. By working together with associations, nonprofits, and faith-based groups, government programs gain more specialized services. They also gain the strength of trusted organizations that help the poor and have a proven track record for success.

Worsening Problems

The problems this bill aims to address are very real. Most of them are getting worse, and none of them will go away without some serious response by our society. That response must come not only from people in need, not only from our government, not only from a few organizations; to make headway, all sectors must participate.

This bill will free up seed money for faith-based organizations that can play an important role in widening our country's efforts. I hope it will also enable these organizations to leverage even more private support for their programs. This bill does not assume that faith-based organizations provide the best services. It is an expansion of rules to allow a level playing field for organizations that were previously prevented from working with the government on social service programs.

1. As of this writing the Community Solutions Act had been passed by the House and was being debated in the Senate.

The intent of this expansion is to allow for a broader range of providers. The previous regulations that presumed providers to be entirely secular hindered and even excluded many religious organizations, especially ones that serve clients effectively.

Providing Social Capital

Given the size of cities and the extent of hunger and poverty today, associations can be more effective with the backing of government capital. If a community-based organization already provides a service effectively, it makes better financial sense for the government to assist that organization rather than set up new programs.

This bill will end the artificial requirement that a faith-based organization create a separate legal entity to provide services to hungry people or those in need of drug treatment, job training, or other assistance. That requirement serves as unnecessary red tape and an excuse to discriminate against organizations that get the kind of results that we are desperately seeking.

As Speaker Hastert said, "It is precisely these groups that are making a positive difference in our most vulnerable communities—working tirelessly on shoestring budgets to help the less fortunate."

Reacting to the bill's introduction, the Union of Orthodox Jewish Congregations of America stated that "the Watts-Hall Community Solutions Act strikes the right balance between ensuring that faith-based social service providers will be treated neutrally, not with hostility, by government grant programs and ensuring that needy individuals will not be subjected to undesired religious coercion."

What the bill does not do is equally important. It does not erode the key principle of separation of church and state or make funds available for proselytizing or other inappropriate projects. Nor does it end federal contracting requirements and other safeguards. Those rules are pretty strict, and I am confident they will protect taxpayers from funding religious activities.

This initiative is not meant to turn social services over to churches and charities in order to remove governmental responsibility. It is a new and inclusive expansion. It does not establish a special fund for churches or allow special favors for faith-based service providers. Like every other provider, they will have to compete for funding.

The government retains the authority and responsibility to choose the best providers. Choices and information are important for clients, for effective social services, and also for faith-based providers, who otherwise may feel the need to diminish their religious character.

What Critics Say

Critics have claimed that H.R. 7 greatly expands the right of religious staffing over and beyond the provisions of the 1996 Welfare Reform Charitable Choice Act.[2] This is not true. What is true is that faith-based organizations taking funding from H.R. 7 have a statutory right to staff on a religious basis. This section explicitly provides that faith-based organizations may take into account religious beliefs and practices in hiring staff.

Under the 1996 version of charitable choice, this was also the law. But the right of religious staffing was rooted in the more general language about faith-based organizations retaining that "autonomy from federal, state, and local governments, including such [an] organization's control over the definition, development, practice, and expression of its religious beliefs."

The charge that staffing based on religion will override state and local civil rights laws is true—when religious beliefs dictate faith-based organizations following their sincere doctrine or creed. The federal courts have not let claims of religious belief allow racial discrimination, however.

Robert Payton, professor of philanthropic studies, has said that "philanthropic organizations are increasingly constrained in their work by legal and even legalistic interpretations of the law. It occurred to me to think of the Good Samaritan walking down from Jerusalem to Jericho accompanied by his

2. The "Charitable Choice" provision of the 1996 Welfare Reform Act allows states to contract with charitable organizations and faith-based charities to provide social and community services.

friend, a lawyer. At the Good Samaritan's first movement to help the victim, his friend the lawyer would grab at his sleeve and say, 'Don't you dare get involved with that!'"

The Failure of the Godless

Hard-core separationists and secularists may try to denounce [faith-based initiatives], but they must not be allowed to succeed in thwarting what promises to be a revolution in the way we do welfare. These faith-based organizations are filled for the most part with sincere volunteers and underpaid professionals who possess an inner calling that compels them to care for the less-fortunate. And they do it more effectively and efficiently than the government. In almost every case, the programs that will receive federal funds already are up and running and have been for many years. They have a proven track record and a demonstrable success rate, often many times that of comparable government programs.

Indeed, the secular-humanist emphasis on the autonomous self offers very little hope for the poor, the sick, the alienated and the addicted. Atheism holds little appeal to the ex-convict who needs a radical transformation of his soul. Agnosticism is not what a single mother of a drug addict needs. Yet, to date, those are the only points of view that separationists would allow public monies to assist. But that mother needs the conviction that she and her child can, with faith in God, completely remake their lives. Millions of Americans believe in that kind of a God and they should not be disqualified from helping others or from being helped themselves on the basis of that belief.

The tired secularist line about the separation of church and state no longer is persuasive. The failure of the godless approach to human problems is evident. The president is doing the right thing by removing the barriers that have been erected between each citizen's required participation in the public good (taxes) and the faith-based programs that have been the most successful in striving toward that good.

Rob Schenck, *Insight on the News*, March 5, 2001.

Because the government is interested in preventing as well as responding to social problems, it should seek to encourage the moral mission of building character and virtues. For this reason, it should protect the ability of faith-based organizations to have a moralizing and transformative influence on those they serve and take care not to reduce such organizations to simple vendors of services that touch only body and brain, not soul and spirit.

Because this bill's purpose is the provision of social services, no government expenditures are supposed to be used to fund sectarian worship, instruction, or proselytization.

Rules for Compliance

Charitable choice also makes provisions for compliance. This assures that alternatives, including nonreligious options, would be available. Removing federal discrimination against faith-based providers of social services will provide more avenues of help for the needy.

H.R. 7 also includes tax incentives to encourage charitable giving. Such incentives can offer a full-scale deduction for charitable contributions to taxpayers who do not itemize (mostly those of middle and lower income). The bill also allows for a tax-free IRA charitable rollover and liability protection for corporate donors.

The Good Samaritan Hunger Relief Tax Incentive Act (H.R. 990) is another charity initiative aimed to encourage donations to food banks. Each year, about one-fifth of the food we produce—about 130 pounds per person—is wasted. The tax code should not block donations of surplus food. As a volunteer at a food bank once told me, "Since government is doing less to help the poor, it should offer incentives for the private sector to do more."

This bill does exactly that by affording donations of food the same tax benefits as given to other forms of donations. That simple change will broaden the outreach to the 31 million Americans at risk of hunger, especially the 1 in 10 who depend on charity to feed themselves and their families. In a time of diminishing resources, approval of this bill would represent an ideal union of the public, private, and nonprofit arenas. It is an easy way for the federal government to empower businesses to play a major role in hunger relief.

Under current law it is cheaper for a business or farmer to throw leftover food away than donate it to the hungry. If just 1 percent of the 96 billion pounds of food wasted each year in the United States went to hunger relief charities, their food supply would be doubled.

Why are these bills needed? The reason can be found in soup kitchens, drug treatment centers, homeless shelters, and mean streets all over our country. In every congressional district, in every community, people are hurting. I have long argued for a bigger push to help them. Through these initiatives, I hope we can widen the corps of people who share my conviction that we must do more.

eeks to change individuals—their attitudes, be- beliefs. Oppressive and exploitative social struc- t intact. Typically, victims are blamed for their While some on the religious right (a minority) accepting government money, their understand- rophetic role of the church omits any challenge rful economic and political structures that cause ate social injustice—which is the very heart of a erstanding of the prophetic role.

ophet" Organizations

of II Samuel is a story that illustrates what happens eat at the king's table"—you forfeit the right to ask r justice (II Sam. 19:28). Government funding of rganizations has a chilling effect on their public, vitness, turning them into "non-prophet" organiza- ee it around us everywhere. There seems to be a di- ve correlation between the amount of funding re- religious organizations and the strength of their all for justice—more money equals less voice.

cepting government money to provide private so- e programs will only serve to deepen the existing nfusion in our communities about who works for has always been the case, and should always be, overnment officials—every legislator, governor, y council member, school superintendent—work cepting government money literally turns that re- upside down—we work for them. The Rev. Dr. uther King, Jr. said it best in the book *Strength to* re he said, "The church must be reminded that it master or the servant of the state, but rather the e of the state. It must be the guide and critic of the never its tool."

nger of this is especially critical for local religious tions that choose to receive this money. Perhaps some non-congregation religious organizations or that are founded for the sole purpose of providing a social service who will therefore not need to be as d about compromising their prophetic ministry. It is congregation that is most at risk of such compromise.

> "*What our cities need is religious congregations that are independent of the influence of government.*"

Faith-Based Charitable Organizations Should Not Receive Federal Funds

Robert F. Owens

According to Robert F. Owens in the following viewpoint, religious organizations should not accept funding from the government. Owens argues that accepting public funds would transform faith-based organizations from independent seekers of social justice to servants of the state. In this new role, religious organizations would be subject to government regulation and would be less likely to challenge the unjust social policies that led to the very problems religious organizations are attempting to address. Owens is a reverend and the lead organizer of Citizens of Louisville Organized & United Together, an interracial, ecumenical organization of thirty religious congregations working together to build their power to address local issues of justice.

As you read, consider the following questions:

1. According to Owens, why was the doctrine of separation of church and state conceived?
2. How does the author describe the "religious right"?
3. List three reasons why government funding of local religious congregations is problematic, as outlined by Owens.

Robert F. Owens, "Separation of Church and State," *Social Policy*, vol. 32, Fall 2001, pp. 45–48. Copyright © 2001 by Social Policy Corp. Reproduced by permission.

When Satan wants to seduce you, he doesn't send you an evil deed to do, because that you will resist. He sends you a good deed to do at the wrong time and in the wrong context, and that will seduce you.

—Menachem Mendel of Kotzk

The . . . debate over whether the federal government should fund "faith-based organizations" to do charitable work is a critical one for both the faith community and for the community at large. However most of the debate so far has missed the primary reason that such activity is dangerous and damaging to both—the chilling effect that government funding has on the prophetic witness of people of faith. I say "has" rather than "will have" because this effect has been known for years. The . . . stepped-up effort by the Bush administration will only make matters worse.

Those speaking out against government funding of faith-based organizations tend to focus their argument around the importance of maintaining "the separation of church and state." Their primary point is that it will be too difficult to ensure that religion is kept out of the social services being provided. In a pluralistic society, this is critical—public monies should not be used to promote any particular religion. Indeed, the Constitution of the United States prohibits it. Those of us who value our freedom of religion—and others who value their freedom from religion—should stand together on that point.

But the doctrine of the separation of church and state was conceived primarily to keep the state out of the church, not the church out of the state. Yet that has been, and will continue to be, the primary effect of this policy—the "church" will remove itself more and more from developing a strong, prophetic public witness in relation to the "state." The shortage of religious leaders who will take the risk of speaking truth to power is critical enough, but it is truly tragic when the development of such a voice is rendered impossible by cozy financial relationships with the powers themselves.

(And by the way, in spite of what some proponents will argue, the mere formation of a 501(c)(3)[1] organization through

1. A 501(c)(3) provides charitable, religious, scientific, literary, or educational services to the public and is an organization that qualifies for tax-deductible donations.

which to receive the fund
no way a guarantee that
vices provided or that the
gregation will not be com
jor point of that are eithe
are being too simplistic
longer even a requiremer
then-Senator John Ashcro
in the welfare reform act
monies directly, which mal

A Prophetic Ministry

Those who seek to follow
that the people of God are
the public welfare, particula
be involved in a public witn
words, to have a prophetic
railed against social injustice
pression and exploitation), e
vulnerable of society—the
poor. And they railed agains
of God had become compli
not-so-subtle forms of econ
and exploitation—by becom
selves, and by "whitewashing
had created it in the first plac

What the prophets called f
God's people to social injustic
but justice. In Amos 5:24, Goc
roll down like waters," not "le
ment funding of faith-based
whammy against the people o
date—it establishes more chari
economic and political justice.

It may be important here to
sion to which I am referring fr

2. The "Charitable Choice" provision of the
to contract with charitable organizations an
and community services.

The latter
havior, and
tures are l
problems.
also oppos
ing of the
to the pow
and perpe
biblical un

"Non-P

In the boo
when you
the king f
religious
prophetic
tions. We
rect negat
ceived by
prophetic

Also, a
cial servic
state of c
whom. It
that all
mayor, ci
for us. A
lationshi
Martin I
Love, wh
is not th
conscien
state, an

The c
congrega
there ar
agencies
particula
concern
the local

It is the local congregation that must maintain its prophetic voice, independent of financial strings that can strangle it.

There are many other aspects of this issue that are problematic for the local religious congregation:

• a wider gulf between those doing the serving and those being served; therefore preventing any real building of community;

• the drain of time, energy, and focus away from other important ministries;

• the threat to voluntary contributions of time and money from their members;

• the invitation to intrusive monitoring and regulation by government into the congregation's mission and finances;

• the creation of divisive competition between sister congregations who are going after the limited government resources; and

• the opening of the congregation's funded programs to possible scrutiny and criticism by any person or group in the country, because the programs are funded with taxpayers' money.

Complimentary Rhetoric

Finally, the religious community should not allow itself to be flattered by the complimentary rhetoric about how faith-based organizations do a better job of providing social services. Even if that is so (and it may be for certain services), that's not the point because that's not our role. The religious community should not allow itself to be seduced into supporting the government's abdication of its role to address critical social needs in a systemic way. Besides, as has been pointed out, if this policy is taken to its illogical extreme, with the religious community taking over from government the provision of social services, then each church, synagogue, and mosque would have to increase its budget by an estimated $225,000 (when the average congregation budget is only around $100,000).

But it's not the effect on the religious congregations themselves that is most damaging in the long run—it is the lost effect on society as a whole. The depth and breadth of the social problems we see around us, which we read about in our newspapers day after day after day, are direct evidence of the religious community's weakness. Just imagine how our community would be different if people of faith would come together by the tens of thousands and demand that the real justice issues of our community be addressed in a serious way.

What our cities need is religious congregations that are independent of the influence of government and can therefore have an effective prophetic voice to hold them accountable to God's demand for justice. What we don't need is more "non-prophet" religious organizations.

> "[Posting the Ten Commandments] will remind each one of us every day that this is 'one nation under God.'"

The Ten Commandments Should Be Posted in Public Areas

Janet Parshall

In the following viewpoint Janet Parshall argues that the Ten Commandments should be posted in public places because they provide guidelines to ethical behavior. She contends that the framers of the Constitution recognized that religious principles reinforce reason and contribute to human morality. She maintains that posting the Commandments would reduce violence and improve society. Parshall is the chief spokeswoman for the Family Research Council, a nonprofit think tank and advocacy group.

As you read, consider the following questions:

1. Which founding fathers does Parshall allege supported religious doctrine as a guiding principle?
2. According to the author, where did the effort to remove God from the minds of people begin?
3. What does Parshall consider the "sheer brilliance" of the Ten Commandments?

Janet Parshall, "Symposium: Q: Is It a Good Idea to Post the Ten Commandments in Public Buildings? Yes: Reminding Citizens That We Are a Nation Under God Can Do Much Good and Very Little Harm," *Insight on the News*, vol. 15, December 6, 1999, p. 40. Copyright © 1999 by News World Communications, Inc. All rights reserved. Reproduced by permission.

When the son of former Israeli prime minister Menachem Begin came to Washington a few years ago he met with a group of friends of the Jewish state. "Mr. Begin," one gentleman said, "I'm a sympathizer. I care about you and your party. I hope you win. But why are you always so negative? I do a lot of public-relations work in Washington, and I can tell you, people don't like negative. Can't you please put your program in more positive terms?"

Benny Begin, who had all of his famous father's charisma and Old World dignity, hesitated as he carefully considered his answer. Then, looking directly at his supporter through thick glasses, he said: "I appreciate your thoughtful question. I will see what I can do. I will consult with my colleagues about coming across too negative. But you will grant us this: In Israel, there are certain precedents for thou shalt not!"

Following Precedent

Indeed. In America, too, there are certain precedents. For 200 years, Americans have like the people of Israel derived their moral judgments from the ideals embodied in the Ten Commandments. Not every American, to be sure, believed that God gave us the Commandments. But few openly question that the Decalogue, as it sometimes is known in academic circles, formed the basis for our public life together. George Washington knew the importance of God's law in the maintenance of civil peace. In his famous Farewell Address, he urged Americans not to listen to those who would strip away the foundations of our national life: "Reason and experience both forbid us to expect that National morality can prevail in exclusion of religious principle."

Those who would strip the Ten Commandments from our national life are doing exactly what Washington warned against. As he put it, "Where is the security for property, for reputation, for life, if the sense of religious obligation desert the oaths, which are the instruments of investigation in the Courts of Justice?"

We have learned to our sorrow in recent years what happens in a country that forgets that oaths are vitally important and that perjury subverts our entire system of justice. Yes, we always can threaten people with prosecution for perjury. And we can put people in prison if we catch them committing perjury. But isn't it better if a person will simply tell the truth, the whole truth and nothing but the truth, so help me God?

Washington was not the only Founder who believed that religious principle reinforced reason and interest. Thomas Jefferson saw an intimate connection between respect for God and the survival of liberty itself. "Can the liberties of a nation be thought secure," he asked, "when we have removed their only firm basis, a conviction in the minds of the people that their liberties are a gift of God—that they are not to be violated except with His wrath? Indeed, I tremble for my country when I reflect that God is just; that his justice cannot sleep forever."

As we face daily examples of horrible crimes—murders, rapes, child molesting—is it really so surprising? For 30 years there has been a vigorous effort on the part of some to do exactly what Jefferson warned against, to "remove the only firm basis" of God-given liberties from the minds of the people.

Start in the Schools

Where does this effort begin? In our schools, for a start. I don't want to refight here all the battles over evolution and intelligent design or to make the case for voluntary student-initiated prayer. Those issues are separate and can be addressed separately. But I do want to say that there is something terribly wrong when a kindergarten girl is ordered to stop distributing Christmas cards to her classmates because they say, "Jesus Loves You." This actually happened in suburban Howard County, Md.

Students are being required to read textbooks from which any references to God have been carefully removed. One example, found by New York University psychology professor Paul Vitz, described Pilgrims as "people who go on journeys." The Pilgrims gave thanks, but the book blotted out mention of the God to whom they gave their thanks. Another example Vitz found, "Zlateh and the Goat," is a story of a young Jewish boy in Poland who is saved from freezing to death. In Nobel Prize winner Isaac Bashevis Singer's original story, Zlateh thanks God for his survival. In the censored version, Zlateh thanks not God but "goodness."

We at the Family Research Council think that the Supreme Court has gone too far in attempting to erect a high wall of separation between church and state. The Founders never intended to put such a wall between the American people and their free exercise of religious expression. We have come to an awful state when every form of vile and vulgar speech is protected and prayer is banned.

We have protested the rulings of the court that banned invocations and benedictions at public-school graduations. The Congress opens its day with prayer. So does the Supreme Court. The justices even look out on a replica of the Ten Commandments in the court chamber. That painting represents the idea that the Ten Commandments form the basis of our laws.

A Higher Authority

We believe that it is a good and necessary thing for Americans to be able to acknowledge their reliance on God. As Supreme Court Justice William O. Douglas—by no means a conservative—said, "We are a religious people, and our institutions presuppose a Supreme Being. The institutions of our society are founded on the belief that there is an authority higher than the authority of the State; that there is a moral law which the State is powerless to alter; that the individual possesses rights, conferred by the Creator, which government must respect."

It was not so long ago that even liberal icons such as Douglas were unafraid to acknowledge the religious basis for our liberties. If there is a "culture war" going on today, it is because postmodernism is in conflict with its own liberal heritage.

And what happens when we forget that our rights come from God? The history of this bloodstained century shows us most clearly. As the new French publication, *The Black Book of Communism*, makes abundantly clear, human lives are swept into the vortex of revolution at an unbelievable rate when human rights are trampled by government. The editors of this powerfully documented work make the case that Nazism claimed 25 million lives while Communism destroyed nearly 100 million. All of this happened because, somewhere, someone concluded that the state was God and had the power of life and death over innocent human beings. That is one of the most important reasons for posting the Ten Commandments in public spaces. It will remind each one of us every day that this is "one nation under God."

A Menu in a Restaurant Window

According to Rabbi Daniel Lapin, founder of the nonprofit research organization Toward Tradition, posting the Ten Commandments on the wall of our government buildings is "like having a menu in the window of a restaurant." The Ten Commandments is an expression of the principles that we support. It is a code of conduct upon which our country was founded; while it may be in conflict with other cultures, it is undeniably a vital part of the American culture. The principles of government found in the Bible are the very principles that have provided the freedoms we hold so dear.

Gena A. Walling and Stephen Daniels, *Findings*, July 2001.

Americans instinctively know this. That's why they support the idea of posting the Ten Commandments. In every poll, people respond that this is something we should do.

Why? Let [journalist] Ted Koppel speak for us: "What Moses brought down from Mount Sinai were not the Ten Suggestions—they are Commandments. Are, not were." The sheer brilliance of the Ten Commandments is that they codify, in a handful of words, acceptable human behavior. Not just for then—or now—but for all time. Language evolves, power shifts from nation to nation, messages are transmitted with the speed of light. Man erases one frontier after another, and yet we and our behavior—and the Commandments which govern that behavior—remain the same.

People Are Not the Law

[In 1999], Americans have been horrified to see violence spread from our city streets. "See you at the pole" worship services have been sprayed with gunfire. Young Christians, among others, at Columbine High School were murdered.[1]

1. In 1999 students Eric Harris and Dylan Klebold went on a shooting rampage at Columbine High School in Colorado, killing fifteen people and wounding twenty-three others.

One of the killers put his worldview this way: "My belief is that if I say something, it goes. I am the law. Feel no remorse, no sense of shame."

There is no better way to remind people that they are not the law, that God gives us the law, than publicly to post the Ten Commandments. A thousand courses in self-esteem cannot compensate for a failure to teach that simple truth. In fact, without acknowledging that God gives us life, liberty and law, it is positively dangerous to teach youngsters such as the Columbine killers to esteem only themselves.

In times like these, it is more important than ever to reassert our country's moral code. That is doubtless why more than 600,000 copies of Family Research Council's free "Ten Commandments" bookcovers have been distributed nationwide. Parents and kids are recognizing the need they have to affirm a law that never changes.

Many people are familiar with the famous wager of Blaise Pascal, the brilliant French philosopher, who deserves to be acknowledged as the father of the computer revolution. Pascal posed this challenge: "If there is a God, and we have worshiped Him, honoring His Word and His Law, we will have a happier life on Earth and we will be rewarded in Heaven. But if there is no God, we will still have a more just and happier life here on Earth if we live this way."

I will offer Parshall's wager: Let's post the Ten Commandments throughout our land. Let's post them in public buildings such as libraries and schools, post offices and courthouses. Let's post them as well in businesses and union halls, in homes and churches. Let's just see if a greater national awareness of God's Law gentles our nature and improves our lives.

"The Ten Commandments are immoral and unfit for teaching to children in any decent society."

The Ten Commandments Should Not Be Posted in Public Areas

Barbara Dority

The U.S. House of Representatives passed a bill in 1999 that permits states to post the Ten Commandments in public schools (the bill did not pass the Senate). Barbara Dority contends in the following viewpoint that the House believed that the document would instill in teenagers the value of human life. However, she argues, the Ten Commandments instruct people to devalue human life by demanding that they abdicate their lives to a supernatural entity. Moreover, she maintains that the government should not try to force religious law on the American public. Dority is the president of Humanists of Washington, an organization committed to promoting free thought and rationality, and co-chair of the Northwest Feminist Anti-Censorship Taskforce, an agency dedicated to the free flow of information regarding sexuality and free speech.

As you read, consider the following questions:

1. What does the first commandment stipulate, as quoted by the author?
2. According to Dority, which modern taboo is tacitly endorsed by the fourth commandment?
3. In the author's opinion, how does the tenth commandment undermine capitalism?

Barbara Dority, "The Immorality of the Ten Commandments," *The Humanist*, vol. 59, September 1999, p. 37. Copyright © 1999 by Barbara Dority. Reproduced by permission.

On June 17 [1999], by a 248 to 180 vote, the U.S. House of Representatives passed a bill permitting states to display the Ten Commandments in public schools. At a press conference, a co-sponsor of the bill, Georgia Republican Bob Barr, said that if the Ten Commandments had been posted at Columbine High School the April 20 [1999] massacre never would have occurred.[1] The bill's primary sponsor, Alabama Republican Robert Aderholt, called it "a first step" in "reinstilling the value of human life."

This ridiculous measure [went] to the Senate, where its chances of actual passage are slim.[2] And I'm sure most readers know that the U.S. Supreme Court has ruled definitively that it is not permissible to post the Ten Commandments in public schools.

So how is it possible that 248 members of the House could do a thing like this? How is it that these legislators, along with more than a billion people across the globe (including, sad to say, many humanists and Unitarian Universalists), firmly believe that the basic guidelines for civil society are encapsulated in these ten biblical pronouncements? Perhaps more to the point, where could anyone get the absurd idea that the Ten Commandments instill "the value of human life"?

Yet it is because of these widely held beliefs that civil libertarians must exert the energy and suffer the frustration of repeatedly countering government advocacy of the Ten Commandments on obvious church-state separation grounds. And that's why I think it's time to change our strategy and challenge the actual content of this and similar proposals involving scriptural injunctions.

Devaluing Lives

The truth is that none of the commandments have anything positive to say about the value of human life. Not only does the Decalogue not teach this, it bluntly tells people to devalue their own lives, as well as the lives of their fellow human be-

1. In 1999 students Eric Harris and Dylan Klebold went on a shooting rampage at Columbine High School in Colorado, killing fifteen people and wounding twenty-three others.   2. The Ten Commandments Defense Act was approved by the House in 1999, but the Senate did not act on it. Similar legislation was introduced in Congress in 2003.

ings. The blatantly obvious and straightforward presentation of this message in the Ten Commandments leaves me convinced that the reason millions of people accept religionists' false claims about them is that they've never read them.

This situation is ripe for correction by freethinkers. Who better to focus the light of reason and common sense on the true nature of religious doctrine?

To begin, then, the Bible itself contains at least two different versions of these "rules written in stone." There are also numerous English translations from the original Hebrew. These deviations present serious problems in and of themselves. To keep this simple, I'll quote the Protestant King James Version and the wording of the commandments as found in Exodus 20:1–17. (A variant wording appears in Deuteronomy 5:6–21 while a significantly different Ten Commandments shows up in Exodus 34:1–28.) And I'll number the commandments the way Christians do instead of the way Jews do, assuming they've been revealed to us in their order of importance.

The first commandment states: "Thou shalt have no other gods before me." Now that seems pretty clear. The most important requirement for living a moral life on Earth is that we bow down before one particular god and no others. But not only does this plunge us immediately into the age-old arguments, pogroms, and religious wars over which god is the "true" god, it instructs us, first and foremost, to abdicate our freedom, our self-responsibility, our very lives to some invisible supernatural entity. Yes indeed, the value of human life certainly resonates in this one!

Killing Art

The second commandment, in short form, reads: "Thou shalt not make unto thee any graven image." But in the Bible it goes on: "or any likeness of any thing that is in heaven above, or that is in the earth beneath, or that is in the water under the earth: Thou shalt not bow down thyself to them, nor serve them." While there are many interpretations of these directives by various religious factions, let's assume the simplest meaning: "Don't make images of anything and don't worship images of anything." Now why should this be the second most important moral principle for all humanity to follow? Robert Ingersoll [a famous agnostic and free-thinker] noted that such a rule "is the death of art." Killing art is hardly a way to promote the value of human life.

God establishes a special punishment for disobedience of this commandment that, amazingly, never shows up in any of those tidy schoolhouse lists of the Ten Commandments. This is a particularly foolhardy omission given the extreme consequences of insubordination. As part of his commandment, God says, "For I, the Lord thy God, am a jealous God, visiting the iniquity of the fathers upon the children unto the third and fourth generation of them that hate me"—this is the stick, followed by the carrot—"and shewing mercy unto thousands of them that love me, and keep my commandments."

Yes, indeed, instilling the value of human life is obviously what's going on here! All the way down to and including the innocent great, great grandchildren of anyone who disobeys this all-important commandment of human morality. What could be more obviously godlike and supremely just than inflicting a family curse on four generations of children because one ancestor created works of representational art and maybe even admired them. And, gosh, isn't jealousy an exemplary emotion for a perfect God to so proudly proclaim?

Proper Decorum

The third commandment states: "Thou shalt not take the name of the Lord thy God in vain; for the Lord will not hold him guiltless that taketh his name in vain." This is redundantly clear: if you bump your head, you must not say "God damn it!" Refrain from "Oh God!" during sex. For extra safety, avoid "My Lord!" and "Holy Jesus!" And for heaven's sake, don't say "Christ Almighty!" We mustn't be uttering any of his proper names in any context other than respectful reverence—since proper decorum here is so critical to the morality of all humanity.

Knowing the origin of this commandment, and the previous one, is helpful here. That origin can be found in sympathetic magic, where an image or name of a person is believed to carry part of her or his soul. Any injury to the image or denouncement of the name is thought to produce a consequent injury to the person. By making it taboo for people to create graven images or to utter curses against names, enemies are denied powerful, secret weapons. Some ancient peoples went further, believing that natural disasters were caused by misusing the names of gods.

Preserving Religious Liberty

When we deal with questions involving the posting of the Ten Commandments in public places, we are not discussing whether we like or adhere to the Ten Commandments. The Constitution prohibits government from getting involved with religious activity, from declaring a state religion or from using taxpayer-financed resources for public displays of religious points of view. The Constitution requires this separation of religion and government to protect the practice of religion from government, not to suppress religious practice. This separation is intended to protect the rights of each of us to believe or not to believe, and to worship, if we want to, in a manner of our own choosing.

The debate, in other words, is not about the Ten Commandments at all; it is about preserving the religious liberty of all Americans.

Jerrold Nadler, *Insight on the News*, December 16, 1999.

The fourth commandment, in short form, reads: "Remember the sabbath day, to keep it holy." But there's much more to it that must be examined:

Six days shalt thou labor, and do all thy work: But the seventh day is the sabbath of the Lord thy God: in it thou shalt not do any work; thou, nor thy son, nor thy daughter, thy manservant, nor thy maidservant, nor thy cattle, nor thy stranger that is within thy gates: For in six days the Lord made heaven and earth, the sea, and all that in them is, and rested the seventh day: wherefore the Lord blessed the sabbath day, and hallowed it.

If the worst this commandment did was promote the silliness of "creation science," we could consider ourselves fortunate. But violation of this commandment could prove fatal.

Throughout the Old Testament, many acts prohibited on the sabbath are specifically spelled out—along with the penalty, which is death by stoning. Numbers 15:32–36 recounts one such case: the public execution of "a man that gathered sticks upon the sabbath day." So every seventh calendar day, you must do no work. Your animals must do no work. Even your slaves must do no work. Yes, that's what manservants and maidservants were—slaves. (This is one of two times slavery is tacitly endorsed in the actual body of the Ten Commandments.) Clearly, this commandment joins the first three in instilling the value of human life!

The Promised Land

The fifth commandment reads: "Honor thy father and thy mother: that thy days may be long upon the land which the Lord thy God giveth thee." The land referred to is the "Promised Land," which was the bond between the "Chosen People" and their God. Therefore, any breakdown in the family, in tribal solidarity—especially if caused by a family member following other gods or marrying outside the faith—could theoretically jeopardize the tribe's right to the land and, hence, its relationship with the deity. So the penalty for such defection by a family member was death (see Deuteronomy 13:6–11).

In Leviticus 19:3 we are told that everyone is to fear their mother and father in the same way they fear God. Parents thus become vice-regents of the Almighty. No exceptions to the fifth commandment are noted, so even severe physical, emotional, or sexual abuse at the hands of one's parents wouldn't alter one's responsibility to "honor" them.

The Shalt Nots

Now we've made our way down to the short "shalt nots" that most people think of when the subject of the Decalogue comes up. These are the sixth, seventh, and eighth commandments. Thou shalt not: kill (unless, of course, God tells you to, which he frequently does in the Bible); commit adultery (which, though punishable by death in Leviticus and Deuteronomy, has been interpreted differently by different sects—given all the philandering by biblical heroes, the polygamy practiced by some of the Israelites, and the use of harems by biblical kings); or steal.

The latter one, like the previous two, is problematic because God doesn't supply any guidelines for applying it. But if we turn to Proverbs 6:30–31, we find the punishment harsh and absolute: "Men do not despise a thief, if he steal to satisfy his soul when he is hungry; But if he be found, he shall restore sevenfold; he shall give all the substance of his house."

The ninth commandment says: "Thou shalt not bear false witness against thy neighbor." If you think this embodies a basically sound moral principle, note the last three words. They make it clear that this commandment wasn't designed for universal application.

Under Talmudic law, only a fellow Hebrew was a neighbor. Indeed, as Joseph Lewis wrote in *The Ten Commandments*, "All the Commandments belong in the same category and were promulgated for one purpose—to prevent injury to the clan and to promote tribal solidarity." One could willfully violate the commandments where "foreigners" were concerned. Even if, by a redefinition of neighbor, we attempt to apply the ninth commandment more broadly, it still fails to enjoin general lying or advance general honesty. This is because, taken literally, it only prohibits false testimony against another person. There is no commandment against lying, per se.

Undermining Capitalism

Finally, we come to the tenth commandment. In short form, it reads: "Thou shalt not covet." But the verse goes on to say, "thy neighbor's house . . . thy neighbor's wife, nor his manservant, nor his maidservant, nor his ox, nor his ass, nor any thing that is thy neighbor's." Again, this only relates to one's "neighbor" (and it constitutes another tacit endorsement of men owning wives and slaves).

But suppose we actually applied it more generally, what then? Why, it would fly directly in the face of the basic underpinnings of capitalism. Where would our great supernation be without that fundamental longing to possess the things other people have? Has it occurred to anyone, I wonder, that obeying this commandment would virtually require the United States to adopt a communist or socialist economic system? Furthermore, this commandment seeks to create and punish "thought crime." But how are we to determine whether a person has actually engaged in this covert crime of coveting?

Well, there you have them—straight from the divinely inspired word of God—the ten moral principles by which all humanity should live, the best and obvious way to instill the value of human life in American youth. Like Ingersoll, I'm amazed at just what a pathetic list of "moral guidelines" we find here and can't help thinking how easily it could have been better. As Ingersoll put it:

> If Jehovah had been civilized, he would have left out the commandment about keeping the Sabbath and in its place said, "Thou shalt not enslave thy fellow men." He would have omitted the one about swearing and said: "The man shall have but one wife, and the woman but one husband." He would have left out the one about graven images and in its stead would have said: "Thou shalt not wage wars of extermination, and thou shalt not unsheathe the sword except in self-defense." If Jehovah had been civilized, how much grander the Ten Commandments would have been!

It's time for someone to say this again. So long as no one challenges the content of religious pronouncements like the Ten Commandments, we'll continue to divert time and energy from important matters to counter the attempts of conservative religionists to force biblical law on American society. The Ten Commandments are immoral and unfit for teaching to children in any decent society. Humanists and freethinkers, of all people, should have the consistency and bravery to say so.

Periodical Bibliography

The following articles have been selected to supplement the diverse views presented in this chapter.

Christopher E. Anders   "Government and Faith-Based Charities: They Must Remain Separate," *World & I*, July 2001.

Stephen L. Carter   "And the World Turned Secular," *Christianity Today*, May 21, 2001.

Mark Chaves   "Going on Faith," *Christian Century*, September 12, 2001.

Derek H. Davis   "Separation, Integration, and Accommodation: Religion and State in America in a Nutshell," *Journal of Church and State*, Winter 2001.

Douglas Farrow   "Three Meanings of Secular," *First Things*, May 2003.

Marlin Foxworth   "Putting Spirituality in Public Schools," *Tikkun*, November/December 1998.

Gary Glenn and John Stack   "America: Fundamentally Religious," *World & I*, December 1999.

Rebecca Hagelin   "It's Not Freedom from Religion," *WorldNetDaily*, April 8, 2003.

Hugh Heclo   "The Wall That Never Was," *Wilson Quarterly*, January 1, 2003.

Krista Kafer   "How to Teach Religion in Public Schools," *World & I*, August 2002.

Roy S. Moore   "Putting God Back in the Public Square," *USA Today*, September 2000.

Rickie Solinger   "But No Faith in the People," *Social Justice*, Spring 2001.

Maia Szalavitz   "Why Jesus Is Not a Regulator," *American Prospect*, April 9, 2001.

Jim Wallis   "Eyes on the Prize," *Sojourners*, May 2001.

Adam Wolfson   "One Nation Under God?" *Commentary*, October 2002.

Cathy Young   "God Talk," *Reason*, January 2001.

CHAPTER 3

Does Technology Threaten Privacy?

Chapter Preface

In 2000 the FBI launched Carnivore, an investigative tool that helps authorities track criminals' electronic activities and communications. Immediately after its release, Carnivore generated intense controversy between civil libertarians, who claim that the technology violates privacy rights, and government officials, who argue that the system is a necessary tool to fight crime in a technological age.

Carnivore was so named for its alleged ability to extract the "meat," or significant information, from huge streams of data. Because the program turned out to be so controversial, the government renamed it DCS1000 in 2001, but it performs the same functions as the original Carnivore. Carnivore is an e-mail surveillance system that is linked to the computers of Internet service providers (ISPs), such as America Online or Juno. Carnivore provides the FBI with the ability to monitor a suspect's e-mail communications, Internet searches, online purchases, and any other activities law enforcement deems important to the investigation.

FBI officials claim that Carnivore is essential for tracking the electronic communications of serious criminals. Communication systems are routinely used in the commission of serious crimes, they allege. For example, according to the FBI, organized crime groups and drug trafficking organizations rely heavily on telecommunications to plan and execute their criminal activities. Intercepting these communications, the government contends, provides indisputable proof of a criminal's guilt. As stated in an FBI document,

> The ability of law enforcement agencies to conduct lawful electronic surveillance of the communications of its criminal subjects represents one of the most important capabilities for acquiring evidence to prevent serious criminal behavior. Unlike evidence that can be subject to being discredited or impeached through allegations of misunderstanding or bias, electronic surveillance evidence provides jurors an opportunity to determine factual issues based upon a defendant's own words.

Civil libertarians oppose the Carnivore program, arguing that it provides the FBI with the ability to view everyone's communications instead of only the communications of the person under surveillance. Thus, they argue, the program violates privacy rights. According to former federal prosecutor Mark Rasch, "It's the electronic equivalent of listening to everybody's phone calls to see if it's the phone call you should be monitoring." Moreover, opponents argue that the program is unnecessary because ISPs already retain the information that Carnivore sniffs out. According to the American Civil Liberties Union (ACLU), law enforcement has been subpoenaing such information from ISPs for years. As stated in an ACLU position statement, "There is no need for the dragnet that Carnivore represents when ISPs have already been zeroing in on legitimate targets."

Several organizations dedicated to stopping Carnivore have been created, such as Stop Carnivore Now. Despite widespread protest, the FBI continues to utilize the program and insists that the program is necessary. The debate over Carnivore reflects how controversial the issue of privacy is in the digital age. Authors in the following chapter debate other threats to privacy that have developed as technology gets ever more sophisticated.

*"New technology has . . . placed all of us in
an electronic fishbowl in which our habits,
tastes and activities are watched and
recorded."*

Technology Threatens Privacy

Simson Garfinkel

According to Simson Garfinkel in the following viewpoint,
technological advances, such as the Internet and electronic
databases, threaten the right to privacy by making private information publicly accessible. Private enterprises, he argues,
collect and distribute personal data, including financial and
health records, for profit. The resulting loss of privacy sub-
jects people to the risk of identity theft and credit card fraud,
Garfinkel maintains. He contends that the government
should enact legislation to regulate the dissemination of personal information and protect individual privacy. Garfinkel
is a columnist at the *Boston Globe* and a fellow at the Berkman
Center for Internet and Society at Harvard Law School.

As you read, consider the following questions:
1. How does the author define the right to privacy?
2. As reported by the author, what was the purpose of the
   Fair Credit Reporting Act?
3. List three responsibilities of a federal oversight agency
   charged with protecting privacy, as suggested by
   Garfinkel.

Simson Garfinkel, "Privacy and the New Technology: What They Do Know Can
Hurt You," *The Nation*, vol. 270, February 28, 2000, p. 11. Copyright © 2000 by
The Nation Magazine/The Nation Company, Inc. Reproduced by permission.

You wake to the sound of a ringing telephone—but how could that happen? Several months ago, you reprogrammed your home telephone system so it would never ring before the civilized hour of 8 A.M. But it's barely 6:45. Who was able to bypass your phone's programming?

You pick up the receiver, then slam it down a moment later. It's one of those marketing machines playing a recorded message. What's troubling you now is how this call got past the filters you set up. Later on you'll discover how: The company that sold you the phone created an undocumented "back door"; last week, the phone codes were sold in an online auction.

Now that you're awake, you decide to go through yesterday's mail. There's a letter from the neighborhood hospital you visited last month. "We're pleased that our emergency room could serve you in your time of need," the letter begins. "As you know, our fees (based on our agreement with your HMO) do not cover the cost of treatment. To make up the difference, a number of hospitals have started selling patient records to medical researchers and consumer-marketing firms. Rather than mimic this distasteful behavior, we have decided to ask you to help us make up the difference. We are recommending a tax-deductible contribution of $275 to help defray the cost of your visit."

The veiled threat isn't empty, but you decide you don't really care who finds out about your sprained wrist. You fold the letter in half and drop it into your shredder. Also into the shredder goes a trio of low-interest credit-card offers. Why a shredder? A few years ago you would never have thought of shredding your junk mail—until a friend in your apartment complex had his identity "stolen" by the building's superintendent. As best as anybody can figure out, the super picked one of those preapproved credit-card applications out of the trash, called the toll-free number and picked up the card when it was delivered. He's in Mexico now, with a lot of expensive clothing and electronics, all at your friend's expense.

On that cheery note, you grab your bag and head out the door, which automatically locks behind you.

This is the future—not a far-off future but one that's just around the corner. It's a future in which what little privacy we now have will be gone. Some people call this loss of privacy "Orwellian," harking back to *1984*, George Orwell's classic work on privacy and autonomy. In that book, Orwell imagined a future in which a totalitarian state used spies, video surveillance, historical revisionism and control over the media to maintain its power. But the age of monolithic state control is over. The future we're rushing toward isn't one in which our every move is watched and recorded by some all-knowing Big Brother. It is instead a future of a hundred kid brothers who constantly watch and interrupt our daily lives. Orwell thought the Communist system represented the ultimate threat to individual liberty. Over the next fifty years, we will see new kinds of threats to privacy that find their roots not in Communism but in capitalism, the free market, advanced technology and the unbridled exchange of electronic information.

The problem with this word "privacy" is that it falls short of conveying the really big picture. Privacy isn't just about hiding things. It's about self-possession, autonomy and integrity. As we move into the computerized world of the twenty-first century, privacy will be one of our most important civil rights. But this right of privacy isn't the right of people to close their doors and pull down their window shades—perhaps because they want to engage in some sort of illicit or illegal activity. It's the right of people to control what details about their lives stay inside their own houses and what leaks to the outside.

Most of us recognize that our privacy is at risk. According to a 1996 nationwide poll conducted by Louis Harris & Associates, 24 percent of Americans have "personally experienced a privacy invasion." In 1995 the same survey found that 80 percent felt that "consumers have lost all control over how personal information about them is circulated and used by companies." Ironically, both the 1995 and 1996 surveys were paid for by Equifax, a company that earns nearly $2 billion each year from collecting and distributing personal information.

Today the Internet is compounding our privacy conundrum—largely because the voluntary approach to privacy protection advocated by the Clinton Administration [didn't] work in the rough and tumble world of real business.[1] For example, a study . . . released by the California HealthCare Foundation found that nineteen of the top twenty-one health websites have privacy policies, but most sites fail to follow them. Not surprisingly, 17 percent of Americans questioned in a poll said they do not go online for health information because of privacy concerns.

Beyond the Internet

But privacy threats are not limited to the Internet: Data from all walks of life are now being captured, compiled, indexed and stored. For example, New York City has now deployed the Metrocard system, which allows subway and bus riders to pay their fares by simply swiping a magnetic-strip card. But the system also records the serial number of each card and the time and location of every swipe. New York police have used this vast database to crack crimes and disprove alibis. Although law enforcement is a reasonable use of this database, it is also a use that was adopted without any significant public debate. Furthermore, additional controls may be necessary: It is not clear who has access to the database, under what circumstances that access is given and what provisions are being taken to prevent the introduction of false data into it. It would be terrible if the subway's database were used by an employee to stalk an ex-lover or frame an innocent person for a heinous crime.

"New technology has brought extraordinary benefits to society, but it also has placed all of us in an electronic fishbowl in which our habits, tastes and activities are watched and recorded," New York State Attorney General Eliot Spitzer said in late January [2000], in announcing that Chase Manhattan had agreed to stop selling depositor information without clear permission from customers. "Personal information thought to be confidential is routinely shared with others without our consent."

Today's war on privacy is intimately related to the recent dramatic advances in technology. Many people today say that

1. The Clinton Administration supported self-regulation privacy policies rather than government-regulated privacy policies.

in order to enjoy the benefits of modern society, we must necessarily relinquish some degree of privacy. If we want the convenience of paying for a meal by credit card or paying for a toll with an electronic tag mounted on our rearview mirror, then we must accept the routine collection of our purchases and driving habits in a large database over which we have no control. It's a simple bargain, albeit a Faustian one.

This trade-off is both unnecessary and wrong. It reminds me of another crisis our society faced back in the fifties and sixties—the environmental crisis. Then, advocates of big business said that poisoned rivers and lakes were the necessary costs of economic development, jobs and an improved standard of living. Poison was progress: Anybody who argued otherwise simply didn't understand the facts.

Today we know better. Today we know that sustainable economic development depends on preserving the environment. Indeed, preserving the environment is a prerequisite to the survival of the human race. Without clean air to breathe and clean water to drink, we will all die. Similarly, in order to reap the benefits of technology, it is more important than ever for us to use technology to protect personal freedom.

The Right to Be Let Alone

Blaming technology for the death of privacy isn't new. In 1890 two Boston lawyers, Samuel Warren and Louis Brandeis, argued in the *Harvard Law Review* that privacy was under attack by "recent inventions and business methods." They contended that the pressures of modern society required the creation of a "right of privacy," which would help protect what they called "the right to be let alone." Warren and Brandeis refused to believe that privacy had to die for technology to flourish. Today, the Warren/Brandeis article is regarded as one of the most influential law review articles ever published.

Privacy-invasive technology does not exist in a vacuum, of course. That's because technology itself exists at a junction between science, the market and society. People create technology to fill specific needs and desires. And technology is regulated, or not, as people and society see fit. Few engineers set out to build systems designed to crush privacy and autonomy, and few businesses or consumers would willingly use or purchase these systems if they understood the consequences.

How can we keep technology and the free market from killing our privacy? One way is by being careful and informed consumers. Some people have begun taking simple measures to protect their privacy, measures like making purchases with cash and refusing to provide their Social Security numbers—or providing fake ones. And a small but growing number of people are speaking out for technology with privacy. In 1990 Lotus and Equifax teamed up to create a CD-ROM product called "Lotus Marketplace: Households," which would have included names, addresses and demographic information on every household in the United States, so small businesses could do the same kind of target marketing that big businesses have been doing since the sixties. The project was canceled when more than 30,000 people wrote to Lotus demanding that their names be taken out of the database.

Similarly, in 1997 the press informed taxpayers that the Social Security Administration was making detailed tax-history information about them available over the Internet. The SSA argued that its security provisions—requiring that taxpayers enter their name, date of birth, state of birth and mother's maiden name—were sufficient to prevent fraud. But tens of thousands of Americans disagreed, several US senators investigated the agency and the service was promptly shut down. When the service was reactivated some months later, the detailed financial information in the SSA's computers could not be downloaded over the Internet.

Laying the Groundwork

But individual actions are not enough. We need to involve government itself in the privacy fight. The biggest privacy failure of the US government has been its failure to carry through with the impressive privacy groundwork that was laid in the Nixon, Ford and Carter Administrations. It's worth taking a look back at that groundwork and considering how it may serve us today.

The seventies were a good decade for privacy protection and consumer rights. In 1970 Congress passed the Fair Credit

Reporting Act [FCRA], which gave Americans the previously denied right to see their own credit reports and demand the removal of erroneous information. Elliot Richardson, who at the time was President Nixon's Secretary of Health, Education and Welfare, created a commission in 1972 to study the impact of computers on privacy. After years of testimony in Congress, the commission found all the more reason for alarm and issued a landmark report in 1973.

Asay. © 1999 by Creators Syndicate. Reprinted with permission.

The most important contribution of the Richardson report was a bill of rights for the computer age, which it called the Code of Fair Information Practices. The code is based on five principles:

• There must be no personal-data record-keeping system whose very existence is secret.

• There must be a way for a person to find out what information about the person is in a record and how it is used.

• There must be a way for a person to prevent information about the person that was obtained for one purpose from being used or made available for other purposes without the person's consent.

• There must be a way for a person to correct or amend a record of identifiable information about the person.

• Any organization creating, maintaining, using or disseminating records of identifiable personal data must assure the reliability of the data for their intended use and must take precautions to prevent misuse of the data.

Reaction in Europe

The biggest impact of the Richardson report wasn't in the United States but in Europe. In the years after the report was published, practically every European country passed laws based on these principles. Many created data-protection commissions and commissioners to enforce the laws. Some believe that one reason for Europe's interest in electronic privacy was its experience with Nazi Germany in the thirties and forties. Hitler's secret police used the records of governments and private organizations in the countries he invaded to round up people who posed the greatest threat to German occupation; postwar Europe realized the danger of allowing potentially threatening private information to be collected, even by democratic governments that might be responsive to public opinion.

But here in the United States, the idea of institutionalized data protection faltered. President Jimmy Carter showed interest in improving medical privacy, but he was quickly overtaken by economic and political events. Carter lost the election of 1980 to Ronald Reagan, whose aides saw privacy protection as yet another failed Carter initiative. Although several privacy-protection laws were signed during the Reagan/Bush era, the leadership for these bills came from Congress, not the White House. The lack of leadership stifled any chance of passing a nationwide data-protection act. Such an act would give people the right to know if their name and personal information is stored in a database, to see the information and to demand that incorrect information be removed.

In fact, while most people in the federal government were ignoring the cause of privacy, some were actually pursuing an antiprivacy agenda. In the early eighties, the government initiated numerous "computer matching" programs designed to catch fraud and abuse. Unfortunately, because of erroneous data these programs often penalized innocent people. In 1994 Congress passed the Communications Assistance to Law Enforcement Act, which gave the government dramatic new powers for wiretapping digital communications. In 1996 Congress passed two laws, one requiring states to display Social Security numbers on driver's licenses and another requiring that all medical patients in the United States be issued unique numerical identifiers, even if they pay their own bills. Fortunately, the implementation of those 1996 laws has been delayed, thanks largely to a citizen backlash and the resulting inaction by Congress and the executive branch.

Continuing the assault, both the Bush and Clinton Administrations waged an all-out war against the rights of computer users to engage in private and secure communications. Starting in 1991, both administrations floated proposals for use of "Clipper" encryption systems that would have given the government access to encrypted personal communications. Only recently did the Clinton Administration finally relent in its seven-year war against computer privacy. [Former] president Clinton also backed the Communications Decency Act (CDA), which made it a crime to transmit sexually explicit information to minors—and, as a result, might have required Internet providers to deploy far-reaching monitoring and censorship systems. When a court in Philadelphia found the CDA unconstitutional, the Clinton Administration appealed the decision all the way to the Supreme Court—and lost.

A Federal Privacy Protection Agency

One important step toward reversing the current direction of government would be to create a permanent federal oversight agency charged with protecting privacy. Such an agency would:

• Watch over the government's tendency to sacrifice people's privacy for other goals and perform government-wide reviews of new federal programs for privacy violations before they're launched.

• Enforce the government's few existing privacy laws.

• Be a guardian for individual privacy and liberty in the

business world, showing businesses how they can protect privacy and profits at the same time.

• Be an ombudsman for the American public and rein in the worst excesses that our society has created.

Evan Hendricks, editor of the Washington-based newsletter *Privacy Times*, estimates that a fifty-person privacy-protection agency could be created with an annual budget of less than $5 million—a tiny drop in the federal budget.

Some privacy activists scoff at the idea of using government to assure our privacy. Governments, they say, are responsible for some of the greatest privacy violations of all time. This is true, but the US government was also one of the greatest polluters of all time. Today the government is the nation's environmental police force, equally scrutinizing the actions of private business and the government itself.

At the very least, governments can alter the development of technology that affects privacy. They have done so in Europe. Consider this: A growing number of businesses in Europe are offering free telephone calls—provided that the caller first listens to a brief advertisement. The service saves consumers money, even if it does expose them to a subtle form of brainwashing. But not all these services are equal. In Sweden both the caller and the person being called are forced to listen to the advertisement, and the new advertisements are played during the phone call itself. But Italy's privacy ombudsman ruled that the person being called could not be forced to listen to the ads.

Government Controls in the United States

There is also considerable public support for governmental controls within the United States itself—especially on key issues, such as the protection of medical records. For example, a 1993 Harris-Equifax survey on medical privacy issues found that 56 percent of the American public favored "comprehensive federal legislation that spells out rules for confidentiality of individual medical records" as part of national healthcare reform legislation. Yet Congress failed to act on the public's wishes.

The Fair Credit Reporting Act was a good law in its day, but it should be upgraded into a Data Protection Act. Unfortunately, the Federal Trade Commission and the courts have narrowly interpreted the FCRA. The first thing that is needed is legislation that expands it into new areas. Specifically, consumer-reporting firms should be barred from reporting arrests unless those arrests result in convictions. Likewise, consumer-reporting firms should not be allowed to report evictions unless they result in court judgments in favor of the landlord or a settlement in which both the landlord and tenant agree that the eviction can be reported. Companies should be barred from exchanging medical information about individuals or furnishing medical information as part of a patient's report without the patient's explicit consent.

We also need new legislation that expands the fundamental rights offered to consumers under the FCRA. When negative information is reported to a credit bureau, the business making that report should be required to notify the subject of the report—the consumer—in writing. Laws should be clarified so that if a consumer-reporting company does not correct erroneous data in its reports, consumers can sue for real damages, punitive damages and legal fees. People should have the right to correct any false information in their files, and if the consumer and the business disagree about the truth, then the consumer should have a right to place a detailed explanation into his or her record. And people should have a right to see all the information that has been collected on them; these reports should be furnished for free, at least once every six months.

We need to rethink consent, a bedrock of modern law. Consent is a great idea, but the laws that govern consent need to be rewritten to limit what kinds of agreements can be made with consumers. Blanket, perpetual consent should be outlawed.

Improving Computer Security

Further, we need laws that require improved computer security. In the eighties the United States aggressively deployed cellular-telephone and alphanumeric-pager networks, even though both systems were fundamentally unsecure. Instead of deploying secure systems, manufacturers lobbied for laws that would make it illegal to listen to the broadcasts. The results were predictable: dozens of cases in which radio transmissions were eavesdropped. We are now making similar mistakes in the prosecution of many Internet crimes, going after the perpetrator while refusing to acknowledge the liabilities of businesses that do not even take the most basic security precautions.

We should also bring back the Office of Technology Assessment, set up under a bill passed in 1972. The OTA didn't have the power to make laws or issue regulations, but it could publish reports on topics Congress asked it to study. Among other things, the OTA considered at length the trade-offs between law enforcement and civil liberties, and it also looked closely at issues of worker monitoring. In total, the OTA published 741 reports, 175 of which dealt directly with privacy issues, before it was killed in 1995 by the newly elected Republican-majority Congress.

Nearly forty years ago, Rachel Carson's book *Silent Spring* helped seed the US environmental movement. And to our credit, the silent spring that Carson foretold never came to be. Silent Spring was successful because it helped people to understand the insidious damage that pesticides were wreaking on the environment, and it helped our society and our planet to plot a course to a better future.

Today, technology is killing one of our most cherished freedoms. Whether you call this freedom the right to digital self-determination, the right to informational autonomy or simply the right to privacy, the shape of our future will be determined in large part by how we understand, and ultimately how we control or regulate, the threats to this freedom that we face today.

"The public has . . . made significant gains in privacy protection through legislation, technological tools, and action in the marketplace and the political arena."

Technology May Improve Privacy

Jerry Berman and Paula Bruening

In the following viewpoint Jerry Berman and Paula Bruening contend that some privacy has been lost due to technological innovations such as the Internet and cellular phones. However, they argue, these losses are offset by recent gains in privacy protection. For example, Congress has enacted legislation to protect privacy, such as the Fair Credit Reporting Act and the Privacy Act, the authors report. In addition, according to Berman and Bruening, technological tools to protect privacy, such as encryption technology, have been developed. The authors maintain that consumer vigilance will ensure that private industry and government work to protect individual privacy. Berman is the founder and executive director of the Center for Democracy and Technology (CDT) and the president of the Internet Education Foundation. Bruening is the staff council for CDT, focusing on privacy and the First Amendment.

As you read, consider the following questions:

1. Cite two examples of how the legal system has laid a foundation for privacy protection, as listed by the authors.
2. As reported by the authors, how did Justice Brandeis define privacy?

Jerry Berman and Paula Bruening, "Is Privacy Still Possible in the Twenty-First Century?" *Social Research*, vol. 68, Spring 2001. Copyright © 2001 by New School for Social Research. Reproduced by permission of the authors.

Without question, the growth of government and commercial transactions and the increase in technological developments over the last 50 years have heightened threats to privacy. Today the Internet accelerates the trend toward increased information collection and facilitates unprecedented flows of personal information. Cellular telephones and other wireless communication technologies generate information about an individual's location and movements in a manner not possible until now. Electronic communication systems generate vast quantities of transactional data that can be readily collected and analyzed. And law enforcement agencies, particularly at the federal level, place increasing emphasis on electronic surveillance.

Gains in Privacy Protection

Confronted by these challenges, there are still grounds for optimism. While dangers to privacy capture our attention, they sometimes lead us to understate the unprecedented gains in privacy protection that have also been achieved over the last half of the twentieth century. In many cases the legal system has laid a foundation for privacy protection through court decisions, state and federal legislation, and self-regulation. For example:

• tapping personal telephone calls without a warrant was not considered unconstitutional until 1967;

• national security surveillance gained considerable oversight in the post-Watergate era; during the Vietnam era millions of citizens were watched by federal authorities;

• important privacy protections were provided for electronic communications in 1986; and

• although records have never been given constitutional protections, Congress has stepped in to protect privacy by passing legislation that includes the Fair Credit Reporting Act, the Privacy Act, and the Video Privacy Protection Act.

In many instances, users of new technologies have taken their privacy into their own hands. They have demanded and availed themselves of powerful new technologies to protect their privacy. And individuals have found—and used—the avenues afforded them by new communications media to make vocal their demands for privacy. New technologies and standards that enable users to protect their privacy are on the way.

These privacy gains can be augmented and many threats to privacy can be overcome if citizens band together for reform and enlightened policy. The hope for progress, in sum, lies in the hands of engaged citizens who avail themselves of the legal, technological, and political opportunities to act in the marketplace and the political arena. Advocates, committed to reform, must communicate that promise to the public. To do otherwise risks convincing individuals that they are powerless in the face of the rise of digital technology and that their only choice in the era of information is to do nothing. Recent history, technological developments, and the action of an informed public make the case for something different: given the necessary legal and technological tools and a clear voice, citizens can demand and achieve good privacy protection. The answer to whether privacy can still be protected is an emphatic yes. What is critical in making privacy a reality in the twenty-first century is the conviction of citizens that privacy is possible.

What Do We Talk About When We Talk About Privacy?

In the United States, the concept of privacy has evolved since it was first articulated by Justice [Louis D.] Brandeis in 1898. His definition of privacy—"The right to be let alone"—has been influential for nearly a century. In the 1960s, 1970s, and 1980s, the proliferation of information technology (and concurrent developments in the law of reproductive and sexual liberties) prompted further and more sophisticated legal inquiry into the meaning of privacy. Justice Brandeis's vision of being "let alone" no longer suffices to define the concept of privacy in today's digital environment, where personal information can be transported and distributed around the world in seconds.

[In the beginning of the twenty-first century], ideas about privacy are more complex, reflecting the rapid and remarkable advances in computing that have made possible both unprecedented monitoring and the unprecedented collection, storage, manipulation, and sharing of data.

Today, when we talk about privacy, we are often talking about personal autonomy as it relates to information about an individual. Privacy entails an individual's right to control the collection and use of his or her personal information, even after he or she discloses it to others. When individuals provide information to a doctor, a merchant, or a bank, they expect that those professionals or companies will collect the information they need to deliver a service and use it for that sole purpose. Individuals expect that they have the right to object to any further use. Implementation of principles of fair information practices—notice, choice, access, security, and enforcement—is key to preserving this autonomy by ensuring that an individual's privacy interests in his or her personal information are protected.

Privacy today also refers to protection from government surveillance. The Fourth Amendment, originally intended to protect citizens from physical searches and seizures, establishes an expectation of privacy in communications as well. New technologies that enhance the ability of law enforcement to monitor communications and compile an array of information about an individual test the limits of Fourth Amendment protections and require that we revisit and redefine our established ideas about this constitutional protection.

Threats to Privacy

Advances in communications technologies over the last half century significantly challenge individual privacy. Deployment of rapid and powerful computing technologies has vastly enhanced the ability to collect, store, link, and share personal information. This ability to manipulate information has played a critical role in reshaping the American economy, making it possible to predict consumer demand, manage inventories, serve individual consumer requirements, and tailor marketing techniques. But to do this successfully, businesses require and use information about individuals, which means that the demand for personal information, and business efforts to acquire it from customers, constantly increase.

Undoubtedly, the Internet has made this kind of data collection and analysis easier and more efficient. Rather than rely on secondary sources of consumer information, or engage in cumbersome telephone and mail-in information collection practices, companies can collect data online, through registration and as a transaction is carried out. Technologies such as "cookies," written directly onto a user's hard drive, enable websites to collect information about online activities and store it for future use. Using cookies, companies can track a consumer's online activities, creating a wealth of behavioral and preference information. This information can be collected over multiple websites, potentially creating a rich dossier about consumers, including their preferences and their online behavior.

Shrinking Privacy Spheres

Government needs to act quickly and decisively to keep privacy legislation and court decisions up to speed. At the user end, wonderfully secure encryption software and anonymity procedures are already available for email, newsgroup postings, [and] Web browsing. These protections need to be made more widespread and user-friendly. Perhaps foremost, however, continued progress towards a more human-friendly society will do more than anything else to guarantee privacy where it's really needed.

A simultaneously more open and open-minded society enables us to shrink our respective privacy spheres. A smaller, more manageable privacy sphere, safeguarding only those issues that remain genuinely sensitive, means more certain protection irrespective of technological advance.

Travis Charbeneau, Mindspring.com, January 5, 2001.

Cellular networks generate data by collecting information about the cell site and location of the person making or receiving a call. Location information may be captured when the phone is merely on—that is, even if it is not handling a call. Both government and the private sector are interested in this location information. While the government seeks to build added surveillance features into the network and ensure that it can access the increasingly detailed data the network captures, the private sector is using this new information to provide emergency "911" services and is considering its potential for advertising.

Enhancements to law enforcement surveillance capabilities also raise serious privacy concerns. Wireless services provide phones that are readily tapped at central switches. Wireless phone location information generated when a person makes or receives a call can be obtained by law enforcement by subpoena or court order. Email messages are in some respects easier to intercept than regular mail. Technology has freed law enforcement intercepts from the constraints of geography, allowing intercepted communications to be transported hundreds or thousands of miles to a monitoring facility. And computer analysis allows agencies to review vast amounts of information about personal communications patterns far more easily.

A Look at History

Although threats to privacy have loomed large in recent decades, advances in privacy have also been significant. If, when we talk about privacy, we mean personal autonomy and protection against unwarranted government surveillance, recent history gives us reason to be hopeful about the future of privacy.

Limits on Electronic Surveillance

In the landmark *Berger v. New York* (1967) and *Katz v. United States* (1967) cases, the Supreme Court ruled that electronic surveillance constituted search and seizure and was covered by the privacy protections of the Fourth Amendment. In *Berger*, the court condemned lengthy, continuous, or indiscriminate electronic surveillance, but in *Katz*, the court indicated that a short surveillance, narrowly focused on interception of a few conversations, was constitutionally acceptable if approved by a judge in advance and based on a special showing of need. Congress responded to these rulings by regulating wiretapping, establishing a system of protections intended to compensate for the intrusive aspects of electronic surveillance. According to the Senate report, the legislation had "as its dual purpose (1) protecting the privacy of wire and oral communications, and (2) delineating on a uniform basis the circumstances and conditions under which the interception of wire and oral communications may be authorized."

In 1972, the government took first steps to address the

collection and storage of information through computer technologies. Elliot L. Richardson, secretary of the Department of Health, Education and Welfare, appointed an Advisory Committee on Automated Personal Data Systems to explore the impact of computerized record keeping on individuals. In the committee's report, published a year later, the advisory committee proposed a code of fair information practices. These principles form the basis of the Privacy Act of 1974, a response to privacy concerns raised by Watergate-era abuses that addressed collection of information by the federal government. Creating the principles of fair information practices proved to be seminal work; they have formed the basis for all subsequent codes and laws related to information collection at the state and federal level and in international agreements and treaties.

Congress acted to regulate wiretapping in national security cases in 1978 through another statute, the Foreign Intelligence Surveillance Act (FISA). In 1986 Congress addressed the challenges to privacy presented by the emergence of wireless services and the digital era with the adoption of the Electronic Communications Privacy Act (ECPA). ECPA addressed wireless voice communications and electronic communications of a nonvoice nature, such as email or other computer-to-computer transmissions. ECPA was intended to reestablish the balance between privacy and law enforcement, which had been tipped by the development of communications and computer technology and changes in the structure of the communications industry.

Legislative Advances in Information Privacy

While gains in privacy protection in the 1970s focused on limiting government surveillance, the rapid advances in computing and in Internet communications and commerce have turned the focus toward information privacy. In the late 1990s, individuals achieved new gains in the privacy of personal information. More work toward legislative protection remains to be done.

Medical Information. In the early 1990s society witnessed tremendous changes in both the collection and the use of health information. The transition from fee-for-service health care to managed care led to demand for unprecedented depth and breadth of personal information. At the same time the environment for information began to move rapidly from paper forms to electronic media, giving organizations a greater ability to tie formerly distinct information together and send it easily through different sources. To address these concerns, the Clinton administration issued new rules under the 1996 Health Insurance Portability and Accountability Act to protect the privacy of medical records. This set the first comprehensive federal standards for transactions that, until then, were regulated by a patchwork of state laws.

Children. Congress passed the Children's Online Privacy Protection Act (COPPA) to protect children's personal information from its collection and misuse by commercial websites. COPPA, which went into effect on April 21, 2000, requires commercial websites and other online services directed at children 12 and under, or that collect information regarding users' ages, to provide parents with notice of their information practices and obtain parental consent prior to the collection of personal information from children.

Consumer Information. The late 1990s brought the first steps toward protection of information collected from consumers online. Efforts on the part of government and business to require that companies doing business online comply with fair information practices represent an unprecedented step toward empowering consumers to protect the privacy of their personal information. In the past, information collected from consumers online or offline was not subject to fair information practices—consumers received no notice about a company's information policy, were afforded no choice about how the information might be used, and had no recourse when the privacy of their information was not respected. Importantly, consumers had no avenue for redress when information about them had been used improperly. The advent of the Internet brought a new focus on information collection practices and new self regulatory oversight.

As the debate continues about protecting consumer information, growing effort is being directed toward baseline legislation requiring companies to comply with fair information practices and to submit to a dispute resolution process. For the first time, we are on the way to investing individuals with rights in their information and with an avenue of recourse for privacy violations.

The Promise of Technological Tools for Privacy

Progress in law is only one area in which privacy has been enhanced in the last century. Applications of technology that limit the collection of transactional information that can be tied to individuals has proliferated, giving individuals tools to protect their own privacy. From anonymous mailers and web browsers that allow individuals to interact anonymously to encryption programs that protect email messages as they pass through the network, individuals can harness the technology to promote their privacy.

Some tools developed to protect privacy exploit the decentralized and open nature of the Internet. These tools may limit the disclosure of information likely to reveal identity, or decouple this identity from other information. Others create cashlike payment mechanisms that provide anonymity to individual users, vastly reducing the need to collect and reveal identity information.

Encryption. Encryption tools provide an easy and inexpensive way for a sender to protect information by encoding information so that only a recipient with the proper key can decode it.

Encryption is particularly important because of the inherent difficulties of securing the new digital media. The open decentralized architecture that is the Internet's greatest strength also makes it hard to secure. Internet communications often travel "in the clear" over many different computers in an unpredictable path, leaving them open for interception. An email message from Washington to Geneva might pass through New York one day or Nairobi the next—making it susceptible to interception in any country where lax privacy standards leave it unprotected. Encryption provides one of the only ways for computer users to guarantee that their sensitive data remains secure regardless of what network—or what country—it might pass through.

The recent relaxation of export laws in the United States should ensure that stronger encryption technologies will be built into commercial products. As this begins to occur, it will be important to educate consumers on how they can protect themselves using these tools.

The Platform for Privacy Preferences. Developed by the World Wide Web Consortium, the Platform for Privacy Preferences (P3P) is emerging as an industry standard that provides a simple, automated way for users to gain more control over the use of personal information on websites they visit. P3P-enabled websites make information about a site's privacy policies available in a standard, machine-readable format. The P3P standard is designed to automatically communicate to users a website's stated privacy policies and how they compare with the user's own policy preferences. Users are then able to make choices about whether to visit a website on the basis of the site's privacy policy.

P3P does not set minimum standards for privacy, nor can it monitor whether sites adhere to their own stated procedures. However, P3P technologies give control to web users who want to decide whether and under what circumstances to disclose personal information.

The Voice of Empowered Individuals

Equally important to the strides in privacy is the voice of individuals.

Using email, websites, listservers, and newsgroups, individuals connected to the Internet are able to quickly respond to perceived threats to privacy. Individuals protested when Internet advertising company DoubleClick's plan to link personally identifiable information collected offline with that collected online was revealed. Negative media coverage, coupled with plummeting stock prices, forced DoubleClick to pull back from its plan. Similarly, when Intel released its Pentium III microprocessor with technology that facilitates the tracking of individuals across the World Wide Web, outcry in the Internet community prompted Intel not only to install a software patch that disabled the technology but also to discontinue its installation in the next model, Pentium IV. Clearly the Internet provides users with a wide forum for discussion and a powerful platform from which to spread their message. Through the Internet and other media, the active vigilance of individuals can and does force the government and the private sector to reckon with a growing and vocal privacy constituency.

Recent history has presented enormous threats to privacy, but the public has also made significant gains in privacy protection through legislation, technological tools, and action in the marketplace and the political arena. Privacy is a work in progress, and more work remains to be done. In particular, baseline legislation to address the collection of consumer data is a critical resource that would assure individuals consistent application of principles of fair information practices and an effective redress mechanism. Industry must continue to develop and refine privacy-enhancing software so that they keep pace with new business models and new technologies. In the debate about privacy, individuals must continue to use the Internet and new communications technologies to make their views clearly heard and understood.

Is privacy something we can reasonably hope for in the twenty-first century? If recent history is any indicator, it is. But whether or not we achieve the kind of privacy we want ultimately depends on whether citizens are willing to organize and act as they have in the past. That will happen only if the public believes privacy is possible.

Equally important is the newfound voice of individuals. Through the use of email, websites, listservers, and newsgroups, individuals on the Internet can quickly respond to perceived threats to privacy. Whether it is a proposal before the Federal Reserve Board requiring banks to "Know Your Customers," or the release of a product like Intel's Pentium III that could facilitate the tracking of individuals across the World Wide Web, Internet users have a forum for discussion, and a platform from which to spread their message. This active vigilance can and does force the government and the private sector to contend with a growing and vocal privacy constituency.

> "The impulse to blanket our public spaces
> and streets with video surveillance is
> wrong both because it will make us less free
> and because it will make us no safer."

Public Surveillance Cameras Violate Privacy Rights

Barry Steinhardt

The following viewpoint is excerpted from Barry Steinhardt's testimony to the Committee on the Judiciary, Council of the District of Columbia, regarding a proposal to permit law enforcement to install surveillance cameras in public
areas in Washington, D.C. Steinhardt argues that public
surveillance cameras would be ineffective at deterring crime.
He contends that studies in the United Kingdom proved
that surveillance cameras simply displace crime from areas
with cameras to areas without cameras. Moreover, he maintains, video surveillance would negatively affect quality of
life by making people self-conscious and uncomfortable in
public places. Steinhardt is the director of the American
Civil Liberties Union Project on Technology and Liberty.

As you read, consider the following questions:

1. According to Steinhardt, what is the real reason public
   surveillance cameras are deployed?
2. List two examples given by the author of how closed-
   circuit television is susceptible to abuse.
3. What is the bottom line regarding surveillance cameras,
   according to the author?

Barry Steinhardt, testimony before the Committee of the Judiciary, Council of
the District of Columbia, Washington, DC, December 12, 2002.

C ouncilwoman [Kathy] Patterson and the Committee, I
want to thank you for the opportunity to testify today. I
am Barry Steinhardt, Director of the American Civil Liberties
Union's Program on Technology and Liberty. The ACLU is
a nationwide, non-partisan organization with 330,000 members and local affiliates and offices in all 50 states, Puerto
Rico, and proudly here in the District of Columbia. . . .

What draws me here today is the knowledge that Metro-
politan Police have been considering the largest, most integrated video surveillance system in the United States. The
decision this Council makes will set a precedent for the rest
of the Nation. It will set a precedent that will have profound
consequences because the eyes of our Nation are firmly on its
capital.

Accelerating a Trend

Video cameras, or closed-circuit television (CCTV), are be-
coming a more and more widespread feature of American
life. Fears of terrorism and the availability of ever-cheaper
cameras have accelerated the trend even more. The use of
sophisticated systems by police and other public security officials is particularly troubling in a democratic society.

As we understand the Washington plans . . . the police are
in the process of setting up a centralized surveillance center
where officers can view video from schools, neighborhoods,
Metro stations, and prominent buildings around the city.
Although the ACLU has no objection to cameras at specific,
high-profile public places that are potential terrorist targets, such as the U.S. Capitol, the impulse to blanket our
public spaces and streets with video surveillance is wrong
both because it will make us less free and because it will
make us no safer.

Here are four reasons why:

Cops—Not Cameras—Fight Crime

The implicit justification for the recent push to increase
video surveillance is the terrorist attacks of September 11
[2001]. But it is far from clear how the proliferation of video
cameras through public spaces in America would stop a plot
like the attack on the World Trade Center. Even supporters

of CCTV like the Washington police no longer press the argument that it would.

The real reason cameras are deployed is to reduce much pettier crimes, such as auto break-ins. But it has not even been demonstrated that they can do that. The United Kingdom has conducted what amounts to a massive experiment with CCTV. In Britain, cameras have been extensively deployed in public places. There are so many cameras that the experts have lost count.

Yet sociologists and criminologists who have studied their use have found that they simply have not reduced crime. The crime reduction claims being made by CCTV proponents are not convincing. Three recent criminological reports (Home Office, Scottish Office and Southbank University) have discredited the conventional wisdom about the cameras' effectiveness. In a report to the Scottish Office on the impact of CCTV, Jason Ditton, Director of the Scottish Centre for Criminology, argued that the claims of crime reduction are little more than fantasy: "All (evaluations and statistics) we have seen so far are wholly unreliable." The *British Journal of Criminology* described the statistics as "post hoc shoestring efforts by the untrained and self interested practitioner." In short, the crime-reduction benefits are without credibility.

The Problem of Displacement

A Scottish Centre for Criminology report on CCTV in Airdre [Scotland] was unable to rule out displacement as a factor, while various studies in other countries indicate that burglars and other criminals will travel long distances to commit crimes. Discussing the justification for establishing a surveillance system of 16 cameras in Manchester [England], Gordon Conquest, chairman of the city centre subcommittee of Manchester Council, candidly admitted "No crackdown on crime does more than displace it, and that's the best we can do at the moment."

"Once the crime and offence figures were adjusted to take account of the general downward trend in crimes and offences," criminologists found in one study, "reductions were noted in certain categories but there was no evidence to suggest that the cameras had reduced crime overall in the city centre."

In addition, U.S. government experts on security technology, noting that "monitoring video screens is both boring and mesmerizing," have found in experiments that "after only 20 minutes of watching and evaluating monitor screens, the attention of most individuals has degenerated to well below acceptable levels."

In short, evidence simply does not support the hypothesis that CCTV reduces the crime rate. At most, what it does is to displace criminal activity to areas outside the range of the cameras. One of the features of current surveillance practice is that the cameras are often installed in high-rent commercial areas. Crime may be merely pushed from high value commercial areas into less affluent residential areas.

Video surveillance is a bad deal for DC's neighborhoods, both because running these systems will be expensive—soaking up resources that could be better used for community policing—and because it is likely to shunt crime away from the monitored areas into the neighborhoods.

A cop not a camera makes far more sense.

CCTV Is Susceptible to Abuse

One problem with creating such a powerful surveillance system is that experience tells us it will inevitably be abused. There are five ways that surveillance-camera systems are likely to be misused:

Criminal abuse. Surveillance systems present law enforcement "bad apples" with a tempting opportunity for criminal misuse. As I am sure you know better than I in 1997, for example, a top-ranking police official in Washington, DC, was caught using police databases to gather information on patrons of a gay club. By looking up the license plate numbers of cars parked at the club and researching the backgrounds of the vehicles' owners, he tried to blackmail patrons who were married. Imagine what someone like that could do with a citywide spy-camera system.

Institutional abuse. Sometimes, bad policies are set at the top, and an entire law enforcement agency is turned toward abusive ends. That is especially prone to happen in periods of social turmoil and intense conflict over government policies. During the Civil Rights movement and the Vietnam War, for example, the FBI—as well as many individual police departments around the nation—conducted illegal operations to spy upon and harass political activists who were challenging racial segregation and the Vietnam War.

While I have every confidence that Chief [Charles H.] Ramsey is an honorable man, who will not abuse his power, times change and leaders change. Massive video surveillance will be a powerful tool in the hands of those who would abuse their power.

Selective Surveillance

We must urge lawmakers to create real remedies when CCTV [closed-circuit television] is used for political surveillance or to target people of color, women, and sexual minorities. Our open records and freedom of information laws will also need to be amended to take into account governmentally organized CCTV campaigns. In short, we have every reason to believe that police will use video surveillance to target those who they think are more likely to commit crimes and even entrap those they believe have a predisposition to criminal behavior. Police recording of persons exercising their constitutional right to speak can have a chilling and intimidating effect.

David Ingebretsen, *Humanist*, May 2001.

Abuse for personal purposes. Powerful surveillance tools also create temptations to abuse them for personal purposes. An investigation by the *Detroit Free Press*, for example, showed that a database available to Michigan law enforcement was used by officers to help their friends or themselves stalk women, threaten motorists after traffic altercations, and track estranged spouses.

Discriminatory targeting. Video camera systems are operated by humans who bring to the job all their existing prejudices and biases. In Great Britain, camera operators have been found to focus disproportionately on people of color. According to a sociological study of how the systems were operated, "Black people were between one-and-a-half and two-and-a-half times more likely to be surveilled than one would expect from their presence in the population."

The racially biased uses of these cameras ought to be of special concern to this Council, which has a proud history of protecting the civil rights of DC residents.

Voyeurism. Experts studying how the camera systems in Britain are operated have also found that the mostly male (and probably bored) operators frequently use the cameras to voyeuristically spy on women. Fully one in 10 women were targeted for entirely voyeuristic reasons, the researchers found.

Once Established, These Systems Will Inevitably Be Expanded

Unfortunately, history has shown that surveillance technologies put in place for one purpose inevitably expand into other uses. And with video technology likely to continue advancing, the CCTV systems will pose an increasing danger to our liberties.

Our visit to the Washington police department's new central video surveillance center suggested that the system currently consists largely of long-range cameras focused on traffic and public buildings that are not suitable for identifying individuals. But the infrastructure for a far more sophisticated and integrated system is being established. Now that the surveillance facility has been put in place, the department will be in a position to increase the quality of its technology and the number of its cameras—and will inevitably be tempted or pressured to do so. Do we want the authorities installing high-resolution cameras that can read a pamphlet from a mile away? Cameras equipped to detect wavelengths outside the visible spectrum, allowing night vision or see-through vision? Cameras equipped with facial recognition, like those already installed in airports and even on the streets of Tampa, Florida?

Video Surveillance Will Have a Chilling Effect on Public Life

The growing presence of public cameras will bring subtle but profound changes to the character of our public spaces. When citizens are being watched by the authorities—or aware they might be watched at any time—they are more self-conscious and less free-wheeling. As syndicated columnist Jacob Sullum has pointed out, "knowing that you are being watched by armed government agents tends to put a damper on things. You don't want to offend them or otherwise call attention to yourself." Eventually, he warns, "people may learn to be careful about the books and periodicals they read in public, avoiding titles that might alarm unseen observers. They may also put more thought into how they dress, lest they look like terrorists, gang members, druggies or hookers." Indeed, the studies of cameras in Britain found that people deemed to be "out of time and place" with the surroundings were subjected to prolonged surveillance.

The Bottom Line: A Lack of Proportion Between Benefits and Risks

Like any intrusive technology, the benefits of deploying public video cameras must be balanced against the costs and dangers. This technology (a) has the potential to change the core experience of going out in public in America because of its chilling effect on citizens, (b) carries very real dangers of abuse and "mission creep," and (c) would not significantly protect us against terrorism. Given that, its benefits—preventing at most a few street crimes, and probably none—are disproportionately small.

"Camera systems can promote both security and liberty."

Public Surveillance Cameras Can Be Beneficial

Eugene Volokh

Eugene Volokh argues in the following viewpoint that public surveillance cameras are useful for apprehending criminals and deterring crime. He contends that surveillance cameras do not violate privacy because the people that they videotape are in public and visible to everyone. While surveillance technology carries some risk of abuse by law enforcement officials, he maintains, the risk is minimal compared with the benefits. Volokh is a professor of law at the University of California, Los Angeles, and the author of *The First Amendment*.

As you read, consider the following questions:
1. According to the author, why are red-light cameras less intrusive than traditional traffic stops?
2. In Volokh's opinion, what is the main concern with public cameras?
3. What are three of the author's Five Surveillance Questions?

Cameras are the hot new law-enforcement tool. I got caught [recently] by one that photographs cars entering the intersection as the light turns red. (My ticket just came in the mail.) Washington [D.C.] is setting up hundreds of cameras monitoring streets, federal buildings, Metro stations, and other locations. Police used cameras with face recognition technology at [2001's] Super Bowl to catch known fugitives.

Creeping Big Brotherism

Many of my libertarian friends are outraged by these cameras—creeping Big Brotherism,[1] they say. But the analysis can't be as simple as "surveillance bad, privacy good"; and at least in some situations, camera systems can promote both security and liberty.

To start, the problem isn't privacy. These cameras are in public places, where people's faces and cars are visible to everyone. The camera that caught me saw only what any passerby, and any police officer who might have been at the intersection, could lawfully see. Nor is this an "unreasonable search and seizure," in the words of the Fourth Amendment: The Supreme Court has recognized that observing things in plain public view isn't a "search" at all, much less an unreasonable one.

While we should be concerned with protecting our liberty and dignity from intrusive government actions, the red light cameras are less intrusive than traditional traffic policing. The law recognizes that even a brief police stop is a "seizure," a temporary deprivation of liberty. When I was caught on the camera, I avoided that. I avoided coming even briefly within a police officer's physical power, a power that unfortunately is sometimes abused.

I avoided the usual demeaning pressure to be especially submissive to the policeman in the hope that he might let me off the hook. I avoided any possibility of being pulled out and frisked, or my car being searched. I didn't have to wonder if I had been stopped because of my sex or race or age.

---

1. Big Brother was a totalitarian leader in George Orwell's novel *1984*. The term Big Brotherism has come to represent authoritarian efforts at total control over a nation or an individual.

And while cameras aren't perfectly reliable, I suspect that they can be made more reliable than fallibly human officers—so I may even have avoided a higher risk of being wrongly ticketed. (It helps that the photos mailed with the ticket showed me in the driver's seat, plus my car's license plate and the precise place my car supposedly was when the light turned red.)

Government Power

The main concern with cameras must be not individual privacy, but government power. Cameras are a tool, which can be used for good (to enforce good laws) or for ill—to enforce bad laws, to track the government's political enemies, to gather ammunition for blackmail, and so on.

In this respect, they are like other policing tools: the guns that police officers carry, inter-department communication systems, wiretaps, even police forces themselves. Each of these tools can be abused, and have been abused. But we accept this risk, because the tools are valuable, and because we've set up control systems that can help diminish the risk.

So we have to consider each camera proposal on its own terms, and ask what I call the Five Surveillance Questions: What concrete security benefits will the proposal likely provide? Exactly how might it be abused? Might it decrease the risk of police abuse rather than increase it? What robust control mechanisms can be set up to help diminish the risk of abuse? And, most difficult, what other surveillance proposals is this proposal likely to lead to?

This analysis suggests that traffic cameras are a good idea, at least as an experiment. They seem likely to help deter traffic violators. They can't easily be abused. They decrease the discretionary and sometimes oppressive power of police over motorists. The big unknown is whether, once the cameras are set up, the data will eventually be used not just to catch red-light runners but to photograph and identify all drivers. More about that shortly.

That's Not Chopped Liver

Cameras in public places—from ATM machines to convenience stores to streetlamps—are also probably worth experimenting with. They can at least theoretically help catch some street criminals and deter others (though we should always realize that worthwhile-sounding crime control proposals may not work in practice). I'm not sure how much the cameras would help fight terrorism, as some people have suggested; but if they just catch street criminals, that's not chopped liver.

More Effective Use of Resources

Surveillance camera systems can enable more effective deployment of security guards/police, be used to assist with evidence gathering by filming both the offender and potential witnesses, and assist with general town centre management.

While CCTV [closed-circuit television] does not prevent public order offences, (which are sometimes influenced or exacerbated by alcohol or drugs etc.) use of cameras can result in a faster response thus minimising the seriousness of an offence and increasing the likelihood of an arrest.

Adrienne Isnard, "Can Surveillance Cameras Be Successful in Preventing Crime and Controlling Anti-Social Behaviours?," Australian Institute of Criminology Conference, Townsville, Australia, August 2, 2001.

These cameras pose some risk of government abuse, from petty indignities (such as security guards using cameras to ogle women) to more serious abuse, such as officials trying to find possibly embarrassing behavior by their enemies. But they can also reduce the risk of government abuse: The camera that might videotape a mugging can also videotape police stops of citizens, providing evidence of possible misconduct and maybe even to some extent deterring such misconduct. And videotape evidence can decrease the risk that the wrong person will be arrested.

Connecting the cameras to face recognition software, keeping the recordings indefinitely rather than just recycling them after a few days, and merging the data in a centralized database would indeed pose a greater likelihood of abuse. Slippery slope arguments are often overstated, but in a legal and political system that relies heavily on precedent and analogy, the slippery slope is a real risk. Once voters get used to surveillance, they might become more tolerant of the government processing the data in various ways. And once the government invests money in cameras, voters might want to get the most law-enforcement bang for the buck by having the police store, merge and analyze the gathered data. This slippage isn't certain, but it's not implausible.

But even if slippage happens, it's important that the potential for abuse is limited and limitable. The danger isn't the government looking into homes, or tapping private telephone conversations. Rather, it's that cameras in public places will be abused by officials who want to harass or blackmail their political enemies.

Making Abuse Less Likely

There are such rotten apples in government. If you think that there are very many, and that law enforcement is fundamentally corrupt, you should oppose any extra tools for the police, since in your perspective the tools would more likely be used for ill than for good. But I don't take so dim a view. I think that for all its faults, law enforcement is filled mostly with decent people. And more importantly, good law enforcement is vitally necessary to the safety of citizens, of all classes and races.

Instead of denying potentially useful tools to the police, we should think about what control mechanisms we can set up to make abuse less likely. And we should recognize that some surveillance tools can themselves decrease the risk of government abuse rather than increase it.

Periodical Bibliography

The following articles have been selected to supplement the diverse views presented in this chapter.

Phil Agre — "Your Face Is Not a Barcode: Arguments Against Face Recognition in Public Places," *Whole Earth*, Winter 2001.

Anonymous — "'Little Brothers' Eroding Privacy: No Secrets: Expanding Technology Has Created a Large Network of Ways to Find Out Nearly Anything About Anyone," *Atlanta Journal-Constitution*, September 5, 1999.

Steve Bonta — "Gearing Up for a National I.D.," *New American*, August 17, 1998.

Tom Colatosti — "The Two Faces of Face-Recognition Technology," *Advanced Imaging*, September 2001.

Barbara Dority — "A Brave New World—or a Technological Nightmare? Big Brother Is Watching," *Humanist*, May 2001.

Economist — "No Hiding Place," *Economist*, January 25, 2003.

Adam Goodheart — "Public Cameras Accost Privacy," *USA Today*, July 22, 2002.

Mark A. Graber — "Surf's Up! Protecting the Privacy of Health Information on the Internet; We Need New Privacy Laws and Better Encryption of Information," *Western Journal of Medicine*, March 2002.

Brad Grimes — "Privacy Matters," *PC World*, May 2001.

Wendy M. Grossman — "I Seek You: Are New Security Technologies Worth the Intrusion and the Cost?" *Scientific American*, March 2002.

Jonathan Kimmelman — "Just a Needle-Stick Away: DNA Testing Can Convict the Guilty; It Can Also Destroy the Privacy of Millions," *Nation*, November 27, 2000.

David Kopel and Michael Krause — "Face the Facts: Facial Recognition Technology's Troubled Past—and Troubling Future," *Reason*, October 2002.

Stephanie Myers — "How Safe Is Your Communication? A Look at Government-Initiated Electronic Surveillance," *Shield*, Summer/Fall 2000.

Solveig Singleton — "Commerce vs. Privacy," *USA Today*, January 1999.

Steve Steinke — "Insubstantial Privacy Losses," *Network Magazine*, August 1, 2002.

CHAPTER 4

How Has the War on Terrorism Affected Civil Liberties?

Chapter Preface

Within hours of the terrorist attacks on September 11, 2001, lawmakers and social commentators were clamoring for Congress to provide new powers to law enforcement to fight terrorism. Despite warnings from some members of Congress and civil libertarians to tread cautiously, Congress quickly complied, drafting anti-terrorism legislation that President George W. Bush approved within six weeks.

On October 26, 2001, President Bush signed into law the USA PATRIOT Act, or United and Strengthening America by Providing Appropriate Tools Required to Intercept and Obstruct Terrorism Act. Many people staunchly support the new legislation and maintain that it provides law enforcement with the tools necessary to prevent future terrorist attacks. Others contend that the new law was too hastily conceived and argue that a large number of its conditions violate civil liberties.

Supporters of the USA PATRIOT Act allege that the new laws are necessary tools to help law enforcement protect the nation from the threat of terrorism. According to President Bush, the act strengthens law enforcement's ability to fight financial counterfeiting, smuggling, and money laundering, all of which terrorists use to support their campaigns. In addition, in Bush's opinion, the new laws give intelligence and law enforcement agencies the ability to share information critical to interrupting a terrorist attack before it occurs. Finally, Bush argues that the act enhances the penalties for terrorism, thereby acting as a deterrent. As stated in Bush's remarks on signing the bill into law, "This legislation is essential not only to pursuing and punishing terrorists but also preventing more atrocities in the hands of evil ones."

Opponents of the USA PATRIOT Act argue that it defines terrorism in very broad terms, so broad that it could conceivably lead to large-scale investigations of American citizens for engaging in civil disobedience, such as peaceful antiwar demonstrations. Antiwar protestors, for example, could be labeled as conspirators in a terrorist plot. In addition, according to many analysts, the bill permits the arbitrary detention and deportation of noncitizens, expands the ability of the government to conduct secret searches in criminal investigations, and grants law enforcement access to personal business records without having to show evidence of a crime. Under the new legislation, civil libertarians argue, the government can eavesdrop on Internet communications and covertly survey records of religious and political organizations, whose privacy rights have typically been upheld in the courts.

These measures and others have elicited a swell of protest among defenders of civil liberties. Protestors of the USA PATRIOT Act argue that the government is in the process of erecting a police state that is systematically eliminating the very freedoms that the war on terrorism purports to defend. When the bill was passed, Senator Russ Feingold, the only dissenting voice in the Senate, pointed out that the framers of the U.S. Constitution "wrote a Constitution of limited powers and an explicit Bill of Rights to protect liberty in times of war, as well as times of peace." He added:

> If we lived in a country that allowed the police to search your home at any time for any reason; if we lived in a country that allowed the government to open your mail, eavesdrop on your phone conversations, or intercept your e-mail communications; if we lived in a country that allowed the government to hold people in jail indefinitely based on what they write or think, or based on mere suspicion that they are up to no good, then the government would no doubt discover and arrest more terrorists. But that probably would not be a country in which we would want to live. . . . In short, that would not be America.

Defenders of the USA PATRIOT Act contend that its most controversial provisions will expire in 2005. However, in February 2003 the Center for Public Integrity, a nonprofit public service organization, leaked a draft of the Domestic Security Enhancement Act (DSEA), or PATRIOT II. The proposed legislation would indefinitely extend many of the USA PATRIOT Act's provisions and further strengthen law enforcement and government powers. The Bush administration maintains that the bill has not been finalized, nor has it been introduced to Congress. However, civil libertarians worry that the new legislation will further erode civil liberties.

Whether the war on terrorism will permanently suspend civil liberties remains to be seen. Authors in the following chapter discuss how to preserve Americans' freedoms during a time of war.

"One would be hard pressed to name a single constitutional liberty that the Bush Administration has not overridden in the name of protecting our freedom."

The War on Terrorism Has Eroded Civil Liberties

David Cole

In the following viewpoint David Cole contends that civil liberties have been compromised during the war on terrorism. He argues that government efforts to identify potential terrorists have resulted in the arrest and deportation of thousands of innocent Arab and Muslim immigrants. In addition, he reports, U.S. citizens have lost the right to privacy, as the government now monitors Internet usage and other private activities. Cole maintains that Americans should remember that similar violations of civil liberties occurred in other wars, and he urges them not to repeat the mistakes of history. Cole is the coauthor, with James Dempsey, of *Terrorism and the Constitution: Sacrificing Civil Liberties in the Name of National Security*.

As you read, consider the following questions:
1. According to the author, what are the most troubling provisions of the USA PATRIOT Act?
2. Why are noncitizens accorded the same basic rights as citizens in the United States, as noted by Cole?
3. As reported by the author, what is the Bush administration's final line of defense?

David Cole, "Enemy Aliens and American Freedoms: Experience Teaches Us That Whatever the Threat, Certain Principles Are Sacrosanct," *The Nation*, vol. 275, September 23, 2002, p. 20. Copyright © 2002 by The Nation Magazine/ The Nation Company, Inc. Reproduced by permission.

From his very first speeches following the horrifying events of September 11 [2001], President [George W.] Bush has maintained that the terrorists attacked us because they hate our freedoms. Hence the war on terrorism's official title—"Operation Enduring Freedom." But [after the attack] it appears that the greatest threat to our freedoms is posed not by the terrorists themselves but by our own government's response.

With the exception of the right to bear arms, one would be hard pressed to name a single constitutional liberty that the Bush Administration has not overridden in the name of protecting our freedom. Privacy has given way to Internet tracking and plans to recruit a corps of 11 million private snoopers. Political freedom has been trumped by the effort to stem funding for terrorists. Physical liberty and habeas corpus survive only until the President decides someone is a "bad guy." Property is seized without notice, without a hearing and on the basis of secret evidence. Equal protection has fallen prey to ethnic profiling. Conversations with a lawyer may be monitored without a warrant or denied altogether when the military finds them inconvenient. And the right to a public hearing upon arrest exists only at the Attorney General's sufferance.

Administration supporters argue that the magnitude of the new threat requires a new paradigm. But so far we have seen only a repetition of a very old paradigm—broad incursions on liberties, largely targeted at unpopular noncitizens and minorities, in the name of fighting a war. What is new is that this war has no end in sight, and only a vaguely defined enemy, so its incursions are likely to be permanent. And while many of the most troubling initiatives have initially been targeted at noncitizens, they are likely to pave the way for future measures against citizens. So as we mournfully pass the one-year anniversary of September 11, we should ask whether President Bush's new paradigm is in fact something we want to live with for the rest of our lives.

Targeting Immigrants

As is often the case in times of crisis, noncitizens have been hardest hit. In its investigation of September 11, the Administration has detained [over] 2,000 people, mostly foreigners, under unprecedented secrecy. Attorney General John Ashcroft has justified the use of transparently pretextual charges to hold them by calling them "suspected terrorists," but his grounds for suspicion are apparently so unfounded that not a single one has been charged with involvement in the September 11 attacks, and with the exception of four people indicted on support-for-terrorism charges in late August [2002], no one has been charged with any terrorist act. Those arrested on immigration charges—the vast majority—have been effectively "disappeared." Their cases are not listed on any public docket, their hearings are closed to the public and the presiding judges are instructed to neither confirm nor deny that their cases exist, if asked. Two district courts and a unanimous court of appeals have held this practice unconstitutional; as Judge Damon Keith wrote for the Court of Appeals for the Sixth Circuit, "Democracies die behind closed doors."

The Administration has repeatedly insisted that it opposes racial or ethnic profiling, but it has simultaneously undertaken numerous measures predicated on little more than a foreign citizen's Arab country of origin. It called 8,000 foreigners in for interviews based solely on the fact that they were recent male immigrants from Arab countries. It has expressly made the deportation of Arabs a priority. And it plans to impose fingerprinting, registration and reporting requirements selectively on noncitizens from a handful of Arab nations. When the federal government takes such steps, it is hardly surprising that state and local law enforcement officials, airlines and private companies follow suit and act upon similar stereotypes.

The most troubling provisions of the USA PATRIOT Act, enacted within six weeks of September 11, are similarly reserved for noncitizens.[1] The act permits the Attorney General to detain noncitizens on his own say-so, without a hearing; bars foreign citizens from entering the country, based solely on their speech; and authorizes deportation

---

1. Enacted soon after the September 11, 2001, terrorist attacks, the USA PATRIOT Act [the Uniting and Strengthening America by Providing Appropriate Tools Required to Intercept and Obstruct Terrorism Act] was designed to enhance homeland security.

based on any support to a disfavored group, without any requirement that the support be connected to a terrorist act. Had this law been in place in the 1980s, it would have authorized the government to deny entry to those who publicly endorsed the African National Congress, and would have empowered the Attorney General to detain and deport anyone who contributed to Nelson Mandela's lawful antiapartheid political activities, because until the ANC defeated apartheid in South Africa, our State Department designated it as a terrorist organization.

By contrast, security proposals that would directly affect us all, such as national identity cards, airport screening measures and the Justice Department's Operation TIPS program, have received far more careful scrutiny than initiatives directed at immigrants.[2] Indeed, at House majority leader Dick Armey's insistence, the Republicans' Homeland Security bill expressly prohibited adoption of either a national identity card or Operation TIPS. Where citizens' rights are directly at stake, the political process has proven much more rights-sensitive.

Citizens' Rights

But citizens' rights have by no means escaped unscathed. The PATRIOT Act broadly undermines the rights of all Americans. It reduces judicial oversight of a host of investigative measures, including wiretaps, expands the government's ability to track individuals' Internet use and gives federal officials expansive new powers that are in no way limited to investigating terrorist crimes. It authorizes an end run around the Fourth Amendment by allowing the government to conduct wiretaps and searches in criminal investigations, without probable cause of a crime, as long as the government claims that it also seeks to gather foreign intelligence—an authority that is particularly questionable in light of recent disclosures

2. The Terrorism Information and Prevention System (Operation TIPS) was a proposal included in the Homeland Security Act of 2002. Operation TIPS would allow volunteers, whose routines make them well-positioned to recognize suspect activities, to report the same to the Justice Department. The Justice Department would enter the information into a database, which would then be broadly available within the department, and to state and local agencies and local police forces. Operation TIPS was eliminated from the final draft of the Homeland Security Act.

from the Foreign Intelligence Surveillance Court that the FBI has repeatedly provided misinformation in seeking such authority in the past.

McMillian. © 2003 by Stephanie McMillian. Reprinted with permission.

Even property rights, generally sacrosanct among conservatives, have been sharply compromised. Under PATRIOT Act amendments to pre-existing emergency powers laws, the President can designate any organization or individual a terrorist and thereby freeze all their assets and criminalize all transactions with them. He has used it thus far to shut down three of the nation's leading Muslim charities. Two were closed without any charges at all, simply because they are "under investigation." The third, the Holy Land Foundation, was designated a terrorist organization, not based on charges that it had engaged in or even supported terrorist activity but simply on the charge that it is connected to [the terrorist group] Hamas. The foundation was given no notice or hearing prior to its designation, and when it filed suit after the fact, the district court denied it any opportunity to produce evidence supporting its innocence.

Military Justice

All of the above measures implicate the civilian justice system. But the Administration's ultimate trump card is to bypass that system altogether for "military justice" a Bush oxymoron that would have impressed even [author George] Orwell [who wrote *1984*, a novel about an authoritarian government]. President Bush has asserted the authority to hold people in military custody incommunicado, without any individualized hearing into the basis for their detention, without access to a lawyer and without judicial review. He has set up military tribunals in which the detainees can be tried, and ultimately executed, without independent judicial review and without anyone outside the military, including the defendant, ever seeing the evidence upon which the conviction rests. And Defense Secretary Donald Rumsfeld has claimed that even if a defendant manages to prevail in such a trial, the military will not release him, but will hold him until there are no longer any terrorist organizations of potentially global reach left in the world, or more simply, for the rest of their lives.

A New Paradigm?

This, then, is the state of civil liberties . . . after September 11. The Administration's defenders advance three principal arguments to justify what they call the new paradigm required by the war on terrorism. First, they argue that noncitizens, the targets of many of the new measures, are not entitled to the same rights as citizens, especially in time of war. This is hardly a novel argument. Sacrificing foreign citizens' liberties is always tempting as a political matter. It allows those of us who are citizens to trade someone else's liberties for our security. But doing so is wrong, unlikely to make us more secure and virtually certain to come back to haunt us.

As a constitutional matter, basic rights such as due process, equal protection and the freedoms of speech and association are not limited to citizens but apply to all "persons" within the United States or subject to US authority. The Constitution does restrict the right to vote to citizens, but that restriction only underscores by contrast that the Constitution's other rights apply to all "persons." These are human rights, not privileges of citizenship.

Double standards are also unlikely to make us more secure. Even granting that it is rational to assume that [terrorist group] Al Qaeda operatives are more likely to be Arab or Muslim, if we are going to identify and capture the few Al Qaeda terrorists among the many millions of law-abiding Arabs and Muslims here and abroad, we need the cooperation of those communities. When we impose on Arabs and Muslims burdens that we would not tolerate for ourselves, we make the targeted communities far less likely to cooperate, and we stoke anti-American sentiments.

The double standard is also illusory, for what we do to aliens today provides a precedent for what can and will be done to citizens tomorrow. When the President introduced the concept of military justice with his military tribunal order in November [2001], for example, he reassured Americans that it would not apply to them, but only to "noncitizens." Yet now the Administration has asserted the authority to detain under military custody two US citizens—Yasser Hamdi, a citizen captured in Afghanistan, and Jose Padilla, arrested at O'Hare Airport in May [2002] on suspicion that he might be planning to set off a radioactive "dirty bomb." The military claims that simply by attaching the label "enemy combatant," the President can authorize the indefinite, incommunicado incarceration of any US citizen he chooses, without judicial review. Military justice has come home. This proposition is so extreme that even the US Court of Appeals for the Fourth Circuit, by far the most conservative federal circuit in the country, has rejected it. Yet the *Wall Street Journal* reported in August [2002] that high-level Administration officials have advocated even broader reliance on this power, and have suggested creating a special camp to house citizen "enemy combatants."

The illusory line between alien and citizen has often been

crossed before. Two of the most shameful episodes of our nation's history also had their provenance in measures initially targeted at noncitizens. The McCarthy era of the 1940s and '50s, in which thousands of Americans were tarred with guilt by association, was simply an extension to citizens of a similar campaign using similar techniques against alien radicals in the first Red Scare thirty years earlier.[3] The same is true of the internment of US citizens of Japanese descent during World War II, which treated citizens as we had long treated "enemy aliens"—as suspicious based solely on their group identity, without regard to individual circumstances. So the fact that we have selectively targeted immigrants, far from justifying the new paradigm, condemns it.

Repeating Our Mistakes

Administration defenders also contend that the "new paradigm" has avoided the worst mistakes of the past, as if that is the only standard we need to live up to. It is true that dissidents are not facing twenty-year prison terms, as they did during World War I. Individuals have not been penalized for political membership, as they were during the cold war. And we haven't set up internment camps for Arabs— yet. But in another sense, we have simply updated the old mechanisms of control. Where criminalizing speech was the order of the day during World War I, and guilt by association the reigning principle during the cold war, in today's war on terrorism censorship simply takes a new form. In the name of cutting off funds for terrorist activities, the government has made it a deportable offense and a crime to provide virtually any support to a group designated as terrorist, irrespective of whether the support has any connection to violence, much less terrorism. Because these laws require no showing that an individual's support was intended to aid terrorism, they would permit the government to prosecute or deport as a terrorist even a Quaker who sent Al Qaeda a book by Gandhi on the virtues of nonviolence in an attempt

3. Senator Joseph McCarthy achieved national prominence and power with his sensational and unsubstantiated accusations against those US officials (frequently in high positions) he labeled Communists. After the Senate condemned him in 1954, his influence steadily declined.

to persuade it to disavow violence.

In defending such laws, the Administration argues that money is fungible, so support of a group's lawful activities will free up resources that can be spent on terrorism. But that argument proves too much, for it would authorize guilt by association whenever any organization engages in some illegal activity. Donations to the Democratic Party, it could be argued, "free up" resources that are used to violate campaign finance laws, yet surely we could not criminalize all support to the Democratic Party simply because it sometimes violates campaign finance laws. And the fungibility argument assumes that every marginal dollar provided to a designated group will in fact be spent on violence, but in many cases that assumption is not warranted. No one would seriously contend, for example, that every dollar given to the African National Congress in the 1980s for its lawful antiapartheid work in South Africa freed up a dollar that was spent on terrorist attacks.

So while we have steered clear of directly criminalizing speech and association—action that in any event is clearly prohibited by Supreme Court precedent—we have achieved much the same ends through the new rubric of cutting off funds for terrorism.

Similarly, while we have not yet interned Arabs simply because of their ethnic identity, virtually all those caught up in the Justice Department's preventive detention campaign appear to have been Arab or Muslim. The government's veil of secrecy has impeded a full airing of the facts, but when they are ultimately revealed, it is likely that many of these detentions will be explicable by little more than ethnic identity. Here, too, the government has avoided explicit reliance on ethnicity for detention, but has used indirect means to accomplish a similar end—the detention of [over] 2,000 Arabs and Muslims as "suspected terrorists," nearly all of whom ultimately had no connection to terrorism whatsoever.

New Threats?

The Administration's final line of defense maintains that unprecedented risks warrant an unprecedented response. The availability of weapons of mass destruction, the relative ease of worldwide travel, communication and financial transfers, the willingness of our enemies to give their own lives for their cause and the existence of a conspiracy that would go to the previously unthinkable lengths illustrated on September 11 require a recalibration of the balance between liberty and security. It is hard to dispute that the world grows more dangerous every day. But that could also be said during World War II, where modern weapons inflicted far more severe damage than those employed in World War I, including a devastating surprise attack on US soil. It also appeared to be true during the cold war, when we were locked in battle not with a small band of terrorists but with the world's other superpower, armed with an enormous stockpile of nuclear, chemical and biological weapons.

Our experiences during World War II and the cold war teach us that whatever the magnitude of the threat, certain principles remain sacrosanct. First, we should hold people responsible for their own actions, not treat them as culpable based on their ethnic, political or religious identity. Insisting on individual culpability not only serves basic interests of fair play but focuses government investigators on the true perpetrators, avoiding the wasteful expenditure of resources on people who are guilty only by reason of their skin color or political ideology.

Second, the government should not be able to imprison people without a public accounting, reviewable in court, establishing that it has a sound legal basis for doing so. The mutually reinforcing checks of judicial review and public scrutiny, reflected in the ancient writ of habeas corpus and the constitutional right to a public trial, are essential to insuring that the innocent are not caught up as John Ashcroft's "suspected terrorists" or President Bush's "bad guys."

Third, we must insist on public accountability and oversight of law enforcement powers. Past abuses have often been shrouded in secrecy, only to be discovered and condemned years later, as when the Church Committee in 1975 revealed the excesses of the CIA and the FBI in the 1950s and '60s. The Bush Administration has sought to pursue this war under unprecedented secrecy, even refusing to divulge basic facts about its employment of new legislative measures to Congress.

Fourth, we should adopt only those measures that we are willing to have imposed on ourselves. Where everyone has an interest at stake, the political process is much more likely to strike an appropriate balance between liberty and security. Where we sacrifice the rights of some for the purported security of the majority, we violate our most basic constitutional commitments.

Learn from the Past

Finally, we must avoid repeating past mistakes. After a terrorist bomb exploded at the home of Attorney General A. Mitchell Palmer in 1919, the Justice Department responded by launching the Palmer Raids, in which thousands of immigrants across the country were rounded up and hundreds deported, not for their involvement in the bombing but for their political associations. Eighty years later, the Ashcroft Raids similarly arrested [over] 2,000 people and deported hundreds—again, without netting anyone charged with the crime under investigation.

None of these principles are new. But the fact that they are old and that they have been forged over the course of many prior crises that also appeared to call for "new paradigms" should count in their favor, not against them. The attacks of September 11 were indeed unthinkable, and the anthrax scare that followed vividly underscored our postmodern vulnerability. But the Administration has yet to make the case that these threats justify compromising our fundamental principles of liberty and justice. In the area of human rights and civil liberties, what is needed is not a "new paradigm" but true conservatism. Only then will freedom endure this operation.

| *"Our efforts have been carefully crafted to avoid infringing on constitutional rights while saving American lives."*

The War on Terrorism Has Not Eroded Civil Liberties

John Ashcroft

According to Attorney General John Ashcroft in the following viewpoint, originally given as testimony before the Senate Committee on the Judiciary on December 6, 2001, government efforts to track down terrorists since the attacks on September 11, 2001, are necessary and effective. He argues that the government's primary goal in the war on terrorism is to apprehend people who pose a threat to the United States while preserving the civil liberties that its citizens value. Critics of the war on terrorism, he contends, aid terrorists by weakening government efforts and dissolving national unity.

As you read, consider the following questions:

1. In Ashcroft's opinion, how is the terrorist enemy "unlike any we have ever known"?
2. What is the purpose of the Foreign Terrorist Tracking Task Force, as reported by the author?
3. As stated by Ashcroft, how does the U.S. government define the term "terrorist"?

John Ashcroft, testimony before the Senate Committee on the Judiciary, Washington, DC, December 6, 2001.

On the morning of September 11 [2001], as the United States came under attack, I was in an airplane with several members of the Justice Department en route to Milwaukee, in the skies over the Great Lakes. By the time we could return to Washington, thousands of people had been murdered at the World Trade Center. 189 were dead at the Pentagon. Forty-four had crashed to the ground in Pennsylvania. From that moment, at the command of the President of the United States, I began to mobilize the resources of the Department of Justice toward one single, over-arching and over-riding objective: to save innocent lives from further acts of terrorism. . . .

Fighting Back

Since those first terrible hours of September 11, America has faced a choice that is as stark as the images that linger of that morning. One option is to call September 11 a fluke, to believe it could never happen again, and to live in a dream world that requires us to do nothing differently. The other option is to fight back, to summon all our strength and all our resources and devote ourselves to better ways to identify, disrupt and dismantle terrorist networks.

Under the leadership of President [George W.] Bush, America has made the choice to fight terrorism—not just for ourselves but for all civilized people. Since September 11, through dozens of warnings to law enforcement, a deliberate campaign of terrorist disruption, tighter security around potential targets, and a preventative campaign of arrest and detention of lawbreakers, America has grown stronger—and safer—in the face of terrorism.

Thanks to the vigilance of law enforcement and the patience of the American people, we have not suffered another major terrorist attack. Still, we cannot—we must not—allow ourselves to grow complacent. The reasons are apparent to me each morning. My day begins with a review of the threats to Americans and American interests that were received in the previous 24 hours. If ever there were proof of the existence of evil in the world, it is in the pages of these reports. They are a chilling daily chronicle of hatred of America by fanatics who seek to extinguish freedom, enslave women, corrupt education and to kill Americans wherever and whenever they can.

A New Enemy

The terrorist enemy that threatens civilization today is unlike any we have ever known. It slaughters thousands of innocents—a crime of war and a crime against humanity. It seeks weapons of mass destruction and threatens their use against America. No one should doubt the intent, nor the depth, of its consuming, destructive hatred.

Terrorist operatives infiltrate our communities—plotting, planning and waiting to kill again. They enjoy the benefits of our free society even as they commit themselves to our destruction. They exploit our openness—not randomly or haphazardly—but by deliberate, premeditated design. . . .

Mr. Chairman and members of the committee, we are at war with an enemy who abuses individual rights as it abuses jet airliners: as weapons with which to kill Americans. We have responded by redefining the mission of the Department of Justice. Defending our nation and its citizens against terrorist attacks is now our first and overriding priority.

The Investigation

We have launched the largest, most comprehensive criminal investigation in world history to identify the killers of September 11 and to prevent further terrorist attacks. Four thousand FBI agents are engaged with their international counterparts in an unprecedented worldwide effort to detect, disrupt and dismantle terrorist organizations.

We have created a national task force at the FBI to centralize control and information sharing in our investigation. This task force has investigated hundreds of thousands of leads, conducted over 500 searches, interviewed thousands of witnesses and obtained numerous court-authorized surveillance orders. Our prosecutors and agents have collected information and evidence from countries throughout Europe and the Middle East.

Immediately following the September 11 attacks, the Bureau of Prisons acted swiftly to intensify security precautions in connection with all al Qaeda and other terrorist inmates,

175

increasing perimeter security at a number of key facilities.

We have sought and received additional tools from Congress. Already, we have begun to utilize many of these tools. Within hours of passage of the USA PATRIOT Act,[1] we made use of its provisions to begin enhanced information sharing between the law-enforcement and intelligence communities. We have used the provisions allowing nationwide search warrants for e-mail and subpoenas for payment information. And we have used the Act to place those who access the Internet through cable companies on the same footing as everyone else.

[In December 2001] at my request, the State Department designated 39 entities as terrorist organizations pursuant to the USA PATRIOT Act.

Removing Suspected Terrorists

We have waged a deliberate campaign of arrest and detention to remove suspected terrorists who violate the law from our streets. [As of December 2001], we have brought criminal charges against 110 individuals, of whom 60 are in federal custody. The INS [Immigration and Naturalization Service] has detained 563 individuals on immigration violations.

We have investigated more than 250 incidents of retaliatory violence and threats against Arab Americans, Muslim Americans, Sikh Americans and South Asian Americans.

Since September 11, the Customs Service and Border Patrol have been at their highest state of alert. All vehicles and persons entering the country are subjected to the highest level of scrutiny. Working with the State Department, we have imposed new screening requirements on certain applicants for non-immigrant visas. At the direction of the President, we have created a Foreign Terrorist Tracking Task Force to ensure that we do everything we can to prevent terrorists from entering the country, and to locate and remove those who already have.

We have prosecuted to the fullest extent of the law indi-

1. Enacted soon after the September 11, 2001, terrorist attacks, the USA PATRIOT Act [the Uniting and Strengthening America by Providing Appropriate Tools Required to Intercept and Obstruct Terrorism Act] was designed to enhance homeland security.

viduals who waste precious law enforcement resources through anthrax hoaxes.[2]

We have offered non-citizens willing to come forward with valuable information a chance to live in this country and one day become citizens.

We have forged new cooperative agreements with Canada to protect our common borders and the economic prosperity they sustain.

We have embarked on a wartime reorganization of the Department of Justice. We are transferring resources and personnel to the field offices where citizens are served and protected. The INS is being restructured to better perform its service and border security responsibilities. Under Director Bob Mueller, the FBI is undergoing an historic reorganization to put the prevention of terrorism at the center of its law enforcement and national security efforts.

State Cooperation

Outside Washington, we are forging new relationships of cooperation with state and local law enforcement.

We have created 93 Anti-Terrorism Task Forces—one in each U.S. Attorney's district—to integrate the communications and activities of local, state and federal law enforcement.

In all these ways and more, the Department of Justice has sought to prevent terrorism with reason, careful balance and excruciating attention to detail. Some of our critics, I regret to say, have shown less affection for detail. Their bold declarations of so-called fact have quickly dissolved, upon inspection, into vague conjecture. Charges of "kangaroo courts" and "shredding the Constitution" give new meaning to the term, "the fog of war."

Since lives and liberties depend upon clarity, not obfuscation, and reason, not hyperbole, let me take this opportunity today to be clear: Each action taken by the Department of Justice, as well as the war crimes commissions considered by the President and the Department of Defense, is carefully drawn to target a narrow class of individuals—terrorists.

2. In the wake of the terrorist attacks on September 11, 2001, several government officials and notable media personalities received letters that claimed to contain anthrax spores. Some of the letters were later revealed to be hoaxes.

Our legal powers are targeted at terrorists. Our investigation is focused on terrorists. Our prevention strategy targets the terrorist threat.

Since 1983, the United States government has defined terrorists as those who perpetrate premeditated, politically motivated violence against noncombatant targets. My message to America . . . , then, is this: If you fit this definition of a terrorist, fear the United States, for you will lose your liberty.

We need honest, reasoned debate; not fear-mongering. To those who pit Americans against immigrants, and citizens against non-citizens; to those who scare peace-loving people with phantoms of lost liberty; my message is this: Your tactics only aid terrorists—for they erode our national unity and diminish our resolve. They give ammunition to America's enemies, and pause to America's friends. They encourage people of good will to remain silent in the face of evil.

Preserving Liberty

Our efforts have been carefully crafted to avoid infringing on constitutional rights while saving American lives. We have engaged in a deliberate campaign of arrest and detention of law breakers. All persons being detained have the right to contact their lawyers and their families. Out of respect for their privacy, and concern for saving lives, we will not publicize the names of those detained.

We have the authority to monitor the conversations of 16 of the 158,000 federal inmates and their attorneys because we suspect that these communications are facilitating acts of terrorism. Each prisoner has been told in advance his conversations will be monitored. None of the information that is protected by attorney-client privilege may be used for prosecution. Information will only be used to stop impending terrorist acts and save American lives.

We have asked a very limited number of individuals—visitors to our country holding passports from countries with active al Qaeda operations—to speak voluntarily to law enforcement. We are forcing them to do nothing. We are merely asking them to do the right thing: to willingly disclose information they may have of terrorist threats to the lives and safety of all people in the United States.

Throughout all our activities since September 11, we have kept Congress informed of our continuing efforts to protect the American people. Beginning with a classified briefing by [FBI Director Robert] Mueller and me on the very evening of September 11, the Justice Department has briefed members of the House, the Senate and their staffs on more than 100 occasions.

Maintaining Civil Liberties

The events of Sept. 11 [2001] demanded swift action on the part of Congress to ensure that the law enforcement and intelligence communities have the tools they need to wage the war on terrorism. At the same time, we must make sure that any new measures do not infringe on the liberties that make our country unique. Congress has achieved both goals.

Anthony Weiner, *American Legion*, January 2002.

We have worked with Congress in the belief and recognition that no single branch of government alone can stop terrorism. We have consulted with members out of respect for the separation of powers that is the basis of our system of government. However, Congress' power of oversight is not without limits. The Constitution specifically delegates to the President the authority to "take care that the laws are faithfully executed." And perhaps most importantly, the Constitution vests the President with the extraordinary and sole authority as Commander in Chief to lead our nation in times of war. . . .

Executive Powers

As Attorney General, it is my responsibility—at the direction of the President—to exercise those core executive powers the Constitution so designates. The law enforcement initiatives undertaken by the Department of Justice, those individuals we arrest, detain or seek to interview, fall under these core executive powers. In addition, the President's authority to establish war-crimes commissions arises out of his power as Commander in Chief. For centuries, Congress has recognized this authority and the Supreme Court has never held that any Congress may limit it.

In accordance with over two hundred years of historical and legal precedent, the executive branch is now exercising its core Constitutional powers in the interest of saving the lives of Americans. I trust that Congress will respect the proper limits of Executive Branch consultation that I am duty-bound to uphold. I trust, as well, that Congress will respect this President's authority to wage war on terrorism and defend our nation and its citizens with all the power vested in him by the Constitution and entrusted to him by the American people.

Thank you.

"Racial and ethnic profiling cannot be the American 'way of life.'"

Ethnic Profiling Violates Civil Liberties

Carl Jeffers

On September 11, 2001, Middle Eastern terrorists hijacked commercial airliners and flew them into the World Trade Center and the Pentagon, killing thousands of Americans. As a result, law enforcement officials have begun to focus on men of Middle Eastern descent as possible terrorist threats. In the following viewpoint Carl Jeffers argues that using ethnic profiling—targeting suspects based on their nationality—in the war on terrorism is unjust. He contends that detaining young Middle Eastern men for no other reason than their ethnicity violates the principles of freedom and equality for which America stands. He maintains that Americans have an obligation to challenge the practice of ethnic profiling as an affront to civil liberties. Jeffers is president of Intel Marketing Associates and CJS InfoConsulting, franchise consulting and information-services firms.

As you read, consider the following questions:
1. According to the author, in what direction will the FBI shift its primary focus?
2. What incidents of profiling does the author cite?
3. Why did some police chiefs refuse to participate in ethnic profiling, according to Jeffers?

Carl Jeffers, "Ethnic Profiling Won't Preserve Our Way of Life," *Seattle Times*, November 28, 2001, p. B9. Copyright © 2001 by the Seattle Times Company. Reproduced by permission of the author.

There is no question that in the aftermath of the Sept 11 [2001] terrorist attacks, America has changed. More accurately, America is evolving—and that evolution is still taking shape as we attempt to cope with the "new normalcy" that we can expect as we go about our daily lives.

Even while the president and his administration have enjoyed virtually universal support and justly deserved praise as they proceed with the foreign diplomatic and military responses to the attacks, the new changes and policies being proposed and implemented in the domestic intelligence and law-enforcement areas have created the most controversy and genuine concern.

Trampling on Liberties

Indeed, many Americans feel we have come perilously close to "trampling" on some of our most cherished freedoms and civil liberties. For them, Attorney General John Ashcroft has become a lightning rod for opposition to many of the new policies and to some key components of the antiterrorism legislation passed by the Congress.

[In 2001], John Conyers, the ranking senior Democratic member of the House Judiciary Committee, held a press conference with most of the Congressional Black Caucus behind him to caution all Americans to be careful lest we see a "wholesale assault on civil liberties in this country."

It is significant that some of our nation's top African-American elected leaders were raising these concerns because, although I don't agree with all of their reservations about new antiterrorism legislation, I recognize that they truly understand the one issue with which I completely share their concern: racial and ethnic profiling.

Information has been shared with the public to suggest that the FBI will shift its primary focus from civil rights and environmental law enforcement and from federal bank robbery and interstate crime enforcement to primarily domestic intelligence and antiterrorism activities. First of all, as upset as I am about the events of Sept. 11, I am still in no mood to see our nation's primary national law-enforcement agency retreat in its duty to protect all Americans under our existing civil-rights laws and to protect our environment from would-be polluters. But if the FBI feels they should no longer get involved just because a 1972 Chevy Nova was stolen and driven across the state line from Ohio into Kentucky, I believe I can live with that.

Washington Roundup

As one of the first salvos in the re-shaping of the focus of the FBI, Attorney General Ashcroft has requested that police chiefs around the country assist in rounding up some five-to-10-thousand "young, Middle Eastern" men to question them on anything they might know about the Sept. 11 attacks. Now let me be unambiguous about my position on this issue. If anyone, male or female, is a credible suspect in not only the Sept. 11 events themselves but also has knowledge of or is known to have had contact with those involved or even associates of those who were in any way involved, then there is every justification to question such individuals—and I don't care whether they are from the Middle East or the Midwest.

Heller. © 2003 by Heller Syndication. Reprinted with permission.

But the essence of the Ashcroft Justice Department request, which is to have Middle Eastern young men come in for detailed questioning without any evidence of any involvement except that they are Middle Eastern young men, is wrong, unjustified, and is at the heart of the most heinous aspects of racial profiling. We must not quietly allow this activity to flourish as a "means to an end," even an end that we all want to reach. That is not what makes America great.

And let no one feel comfortable or "safe" simply because this time, it's not their group. All Americans know the history of profiling both in our great country and throughout the world, and we must continue to represent the highest ideals for which this country stands and for which Americans— white, black, Jewish, Catholic, Asian and Americans of Middle Eastern descent—have also died for. Whether it was the terrible pogroms in Europe and Russia of the 19th and early 20th centuries that targeted Jews or whether it was politically sanctioned anti-Catholic profiling right here at home in the 1800s, Americans understand that we as a great nation of free people have an obligation to be better than that.

Civil Disobedience

Some police chiefs around the country certainly understand this point. [In November 2001], several of them have informed the Justice Department that they will not participate in rounding up Middle Eastern young men to detain and question them with no basis or credible evidence to justify such actions. And their reasons include not only moral discomfort but also the hard fact that police departments have been losing racial-profiling lawsuits on a regular basis.

President [George W.] Bush says we are fighting the war on terrorism to "protect our American freedoms" and preserve our "way of life." I expect him to do exactly that. Racial and ethnic profiling cannot be the American "way of life." Indeed, before Sept. 11, that was one aspect of the American "way of life" we were fighting against. Even in the "new normalcy," that must not change.

"Common sense demands the use of profiling if the United States is going to have any chance to prevent . . . terrorist atrocities in the future."

Ethnic Profiling Is Necessary

Bruce J. Terris

On September 11, 2001, Middle Eastern terrorists commandeered commercial airplanes and flew them into the World Trade Center and the Pentagon, killing thousands. In response, those responsible for preventing further attacks have begun focusing on young men of Middle Eastern heritage as potential terrorists. In the following viewpoint Bruce J. Terris argues that ethnic profiling—targeting suspects based on their ethnicity—in the war on terrorism is an effective tool for preventing terrorist attacks. He contends that randomly searching people at airports who are unlikely to be terrorists—eighty-year-old African American women, for example—is ineffective. He maintains that focusing on the people who are most likely to present a safety risk—young, Middle Eastern men—is the best way to prevent future terrorist attacks. Terris is an attorney who practices in Washington, D.C.

As you read, consider the following questions:

1. How do the police use ethnic profiling, according to Terris?
2. In the author's opinion, how has Israel avoided large-scale attacks like the one that occurred in the United States on September 11, 2001?
3. As stated by Terris, how can racial profiling be abused?

Bruce J. Terris, "Common Sense in Profiling," *Midstream*, vol. 48, February/March 2002, pp. 11–12. Copyright © 2002 by the Theodor Herzl Foundation. Reproduced by permission.

A few days after [the September 11, 2001, terrorist attacks], passengers or pilots on several flights refused to fly when they saw several Arabs about to board the planes. They were roundly condemned by officialdom and the press. But they were right. They were using common sense. They were simply doing basic "profiling," determining that future terrorist actions were also likely to be carried out by Arab males.

I am not going to discuss court decisions that have considered the profiling of minorities. I am not doing so because I have faith in American courts interpreting the Constitution consistent with common sense. And, as I will discuss, common sense demands the use of profiling if the United States is going to have any chance to prevent or at least reduce the number of terrorist atrocities in the future.

Profiling in Police Work

The police use profiling as a matter of course. Let me give an example. If eyewitnesses describe bank robbers as being Arabs, the police will, of course, in looking for the criminals, naturally concentrate their attention on Arabs. However, since the eyewitnesses may be wrong, competent policemen will not devote all their resources to investigating Arabs. But they will proportionally stop far more Arabs at roadblocks than non-Arabs, look for likely criminals in the Arab community, and describe the likely criminals as Arabs to the media so that the public can be alerted to help find them.

I assume that no one would object to this profiling, since it is based on concrete evidence that the bank robbers were probably Arabs. However, the evidence is just as strong that future terrorist attacks are likely to be committed by Arabs. All nineteen of the hijackers who crashed the four planes on September 11th were Arabs. The suspects who have since been picked up by the FBI are entirely or at least mostly Arabs. The terrorist attacks against Americans, which cost hundreds of lives during the last decade in Lebanon, Saudi Arabia, Kenya, Tanzania, and Yemen, have all been carried out by Arabs. The Arab terrorist organization run by, [Osama] bin Laden has openly stated that it intends to continue with its terrorism against the United States. One has to be politically correct to the point of blindness not to believe that future attacks are likely be carried out by Arabs.

This, of course, does not mean that other sources should be ignored. It is possible that Arabs will recruit non-Arabs to do their dirty work, that non-Arab terrorist organizations in places like Spain and South America will be encouraged by the events of September 11th to commit terrorism in the United States, or that home-grown ideologues like Timothy McVeigh[1] or crackpots will engage in terrorism. But these possibilities are far less likely or are at least far less likely to have the incredible results of September 11th.

Learning from Israel

The experience of Israel in combating terrorism shows what needs to be done in this country. Israel has been the number one target of Arab terrorists for decades, but no Israeli plane has ever been hijacked, and no other terrorist acts have ever resulted in anything close to the loss of life that occurred on September 11th. The reason customarily given for this success is the tight security in Ben Gurion Airport.

I have flown out of Ben Gurion more than 150 times in the last 20 years. The Israeli success does not come from using scanners or asking the usual questions—did you pack this bag yourself, and has it been under your control since you packed it? Instead, the heart of the Israeli system is that they profile. They concentrate their attention on the people that they believe are likely to be most dangerous.

The Israelis use intelligent and well-trained security to question all passengers, not sales representatives who handle check-in at airline counters. Based on profiling, some passengers are questioned for only a couple of minutes. Others, who appear more suspicious, may be questioned for 15 to 30 minutes. A few have their hand- and checked-luggage searched from top to bottom.

The Israeli criteria for profiling have not, for obvious reasons, been published. But it is obvious, from my watching the proceedings in Ben Gurion so many times, that Israelis other than Arabs are questioned for only a couple of minutes, and

1. Timothy McVeigh was convicted of bombing the Oklahoma City Federal Building in 1995. One hundred forty-nine adults and nineteen children were killed in the blast.

their luggage is rarely checked. A small number of Americans and Europeans, who satisfy some criteria for suspicion, are questioned longer, and a very few have their hand-luggage searched. In contrast, virtually all Arabs are thoroughly questioned and their luggage carefully gone through.

Realistic Delays

Several times, the *Washington Post* has reported that the United States could never adopt the Israeli approach, because passengers in Israel are delayed for 45 minutes or more going through security and the delay would be worse in the busy airports of the United States. However, it has never taken me more than 10 minutes to go through security at Ben Gurion, including the time waiting to be questioned. I have seen very few other passengers waiting for longer than 10 or 15 minutes. The few exceptions are passengers who fall within the suspect categories. The process takes so little time, because the Israelis have enough security personnel to handle the number of passengers boarding the particular plane and the operation is efficiently organized. There is no reason why the United States cannot run just as efficient and effective operations if it chooses to do so.

In comparison, not long ago I took a flight from Reagan National Airport to Newark to Tel Aviv. On the domestic flight to Newark, my checked-luggage was run through a scanner, but only because I was flying to Israel. The checked-luggage of none of the other passengers was scanned. Hand-luggage belonging to only two of the approximately 50 passengers was examined by security personnel. The choice was made arbitrarily, by computer. As it happened, I was chosen. So after 150 flights to and from Israel and the United States, my hand-luggage was finally searched, not at Ben Gurion but in Washington, D.C. I would have had no objection, except that I know that such arbitrary decision-making is totally ineffective to guard against terrorists.

In contrast, before the flight from Newark to Tel Aviv, the hand-luggage of every passenger was carefully checked, and a wand and pat-down were used on the person of every passenger. This took almost an hour. This system is admirably effective. However, this is not done on domestic flights, like the ones that were used to crash planes into the World Trade Center, and it is probably not going to continue, even for most international flights, in view of the cost and delay.

Commonsense Profiling

No one likes to say it out loud, but more than half the people on the FBI's Most Wanted terrorist list are named Mohammed, Ahmed, or both (for instance, Ahmed Mohammed Hamed Ali). Islamic terrorists will necessarily be Muslims, and probably from the Arab world. Not to profile for those characteristics is simply to ignore the nature of today's terrorism. As security expert Neil Livingstone points out, when the Black Panthers were hijacking planes in the 1970s, security personnel should have been on the lookout for young black men; when D.B. Cooper—the famed skyjacker who parachuted out of a plane with a bagful of cash in 1971—was on the public mind, security should have been suspicious of young-to-middle-aged white men booked to fly over rugged terrain.

Richard Lowry, *National Review*, January 28, 2002.

Existing luggage scanners, even the new improved varieties, cannot detect every weapon, every explosive material, and every other dangerous object. Yet, it is obvious that American airports are not going to search carefully the luggage and person of every passenger. If every piece of luggage and every passenger were carefully searched, the cost would be astronomical and the delay prohibitive. The only alternatives are to check nobody, to check a few passengers arbitrarily, or to attempt to choose rationally the passengers who present the greatest danger.

In light of the events of September 11th, we can obviously not afford to check nobody. If we check passengers arbitrarily, we will waste precious resources checking blacks, Hispanics, and Norwegians, even though experience tells us that they are extremely unlikely to be hijackers. We will check 80-year-old women and 8-year-old children. It would be pure luck if we happened to check the actual terrorists. On the other hand, if experts establish rational profiling criteria, we can concentrate our efforts on the categories of passengers likely to be dangerous.

The issue of profiling does not apply only to airplane

flights. Terrorism experts warn that future terrorist attacks may involve trucks loaded with explosives, as in the attacks in Kenya and Tanzania. As a result, for one day, the police checked every truck going through the Baltimore Harbor Tunnel. When massive traffic jams developed, the effort was abandoned. Now, only spot checks are being made. But profiling is not being done to concentrate on the truck drivers likely to pose the greatest danger. Similarly, vehicles crossing the border from Canada are either being checked carefully, causing massive lines, or are not being checked at all.

It is argued that no government actions in the United States should be based on ethnicity, or race, or religion. However, as the bank robbery example set forth above shows, law enforcement agencies regularly profile in order to solve crimes, even though they may not use this term. The terrorist danger now facing the United States is far more serious than any bank robbery or other criminal acts against which profiling is now being used.

No doubt, profiling can be abused. It can be used for crimes that are not serious enough to justify the use of ethnic or racial criteria. It can be used when its basis is simple bigotry. But virtually any law enforcement technique that is appropriate for some situations can be used illegally or immorally in other situations. The only remedy for such abuse is constant vigilance by higher government officials, the media, and the public to assure that profiling is only used when it is appropriate to do so. The danger from terrorism in the United States is now so grave and so clear that the need for profiling easily satisfies any such standard.

Political correctness cannot be allowed to divert this country away from targeting in airports and other dangerous situations the people most likely to be terrorists. We should not be wasting time, and effort, and money checking people who almost certainly are not dangerous, just so we can pretend that we are treating all people alike. Should we really check carefully 80-year-old black grandmothers, so we can say that we are not singling out 25-year-old Arabs? The answer is so obvious that it is only common sense.

Periodical Bibliography

The following articles have been selected to supplement the diverse views presented in this chapter.

Matt Bowles — "The State, Power, and Resistance: Organizing for Our Civil Liberties," *Left Turn*, May/June 2003.

David M. Brown — "The State's Quest for Total Information Awareness," *Ideas on Liberty*, May 2003.

David Cole — "Patriot Act's Big Brother," *Nation*, March 17, 2003.

Valerie L. Demmer — "Civil Liberties and Homeland Security," *Humanist*, January/February 2002.

James X. Dempsey — "Civil Liberties in a Time of Crisis," *Human Rights*, January 1, 2002.

Economist — "A Question of Freedom," *Economist*, March 8, 2003.

Nick Gillespie — "Freedom for Safety: An Old Trade—and a Useless One," *Reason*, October 2002.

Anthony Lewis — "First They Came for the Muslims . . . : The Justice Department's War on Immigrants," *American Prospect*, March 2003.

Richard Lowry — "Profiles in Cowardice: How to Deal with the Terrorist Threat—and How Not To," *National Review*, January 28, 2002.

Michael I. Niman — "Indefinite Detention and Other Tales from the New America," *Humanist*, September/October 2002.

Ron Paul — "A Constitutional Response," *Liberty*, December 2001.

Stuart Taylor — "The Case for Using Racial Profiling at Airports," *National Journal*, September 22, 2001.

Laurence H. Tribe — "We Can Strike a Balance on Civil Liberties," *Wall Street Journal*, September 27, 2001.

Erika Waak — "The Global Reach of Privacy Invasion," *Humanist*, November/December 2002.

Joshua Zeitz — "Are Our Liberties in Peril? Facing a Nearly Invisible Enemy, We All May Be Subjected to New Kinds of Government Scrutiny. But Past Wars Suggest the Final Result May Be Greater Freedom," *American Heritage*, November/December 2001.

For Further Discussion

Chapter 1

1. Francis Canavan argues that free expression is only valuable when it contributes to the good of society. The American Civil Liberties Union (ACLU) contends that free expression is always essential because it ensures the free exchange of ideas. With whose argument do you most agree? Citing from the texts, explain your answer.

2. According to Laura Leets, hate speech should be regulated because it may contribute to the rising incidence of hate crimes. Ted Gup maintains that hate speech should not be limited because open discussion of hateful ideas is critical to reducing bigotry in society. In your opinion, does hate speech contribute to violent crime? Or, do you think that hate speech performs a valuable function in society? Why or why not?

3. Shawntel Smith asserts that desecrating the flag rejects the values that it represents: freedom, opportunity, and unity. Andrew Cohen argues that flags are personal property, and the values represented by the flag are not harmed by a person damaging his or her own property. Whose argument do you find most convincing and why?

4. According to Paul M. Rodriguez, virtual child pornography should be banned because it may incite pedophiles to molest young children. Wendy Kaminer contends that because virtual child pornography is computer-generated pictures of children engaged in sex acts, no children were harmed in the making of it. Thus, she argues, virtual child pornography is protected free speech. Based on the authors' arguments, do you think that virtual child pornography is a form of speech that should be protected? Why or why not?

Chapter 2

1. Alan Wolfe argues that the separation of church and state is necessary to prevent a nation's major religion from dominating the government and subordinating minor faiths. Steve Bonta contends that completely separating church and state is impossible because government exists to protect God-given individual rights. Which author makes a stronger case? Support your answer with evidence from the viewpoints.

2. Tony Hall contends that religious organizations should be eligible for public funds because they perform public services. In Robert F. Owens's opinion, accepting public funds, and, in turn,

accepting government regulation, would compromise faith-based organizations' ability to challenge unjust social policies. Based on your reading of the viewpoints, do you think that faith-based charity organizations should receive public funds? Why or why not?

3. In Janet Parshall's opinion the Ten Commandments should be posted in public areas because they provide guidelines to ethical behavior. Barbara Dority argues that the Ten Commandments are immoral guidelines that demand subjugation to a religious authority. How do Parshall's and Dority's differing views on the Ten Commandments reflect their beliefs about the separation of church and state?

Chapter 3

1. According to Simson Garfinkel, technological advances such as the Internet have jeopardized Americans' right to privacy. Jerry Berman and Paula Bruening contend that some privacy has been lost to technology, but they assert that these losses are offset by technological innovations in privacy protection. Whose argument do you find most convincing and why?

2. Barry Steinhardt asserts that public surveillance cameras violate privacy rights and are ineffective at deterring crime. Eugene Volokh argues that public surveillance cameras pose some risk to privacy rights, but their usefulness at reducing crime outweighs the small loss of privacy. Based on your reading of the viewpoints, do you think that public surveillance cameras threaten the right to privacy? Why or why not?

Chapter 4

1. David Cole argues that the war on terrorism has eroded privacy rights and unfairly targeted Muslim immigrants. John Ashcroft maintains that the government has taken the necessary steps to preserve civil liberties during the war on terrorism. In your opinion, have the increased security measures Cole and Ashcroft discuss been too draconian? Citing from the texts, explain why or why not.

2. Carl Jeffers argues that targeting young men of Middle Eastern origin as possible terrorists is unfair. Bruce J. Terris maintains that the most effective way to prevent recurrences of the September 11, 2001, terrorist attacks is to closely monitor the people most likely to carry out similar attacks—young men of Middle Eastern origin. Whose evidence do you find most compelling? Do you think ethnic profiling violates civil liberties? Explain your answer using evidence from the texts.

Organizations to Contact

The editors have compiled the following list of organizations concerned with the issues debated in this book. The descriptions are derived from materials provided by the organizations. All have publications or information available for interested readers. The list was compiled on the date of publication of the present volume; the information provided here may change. Be aware that many organizations take several weeks or longer to respond to inquiries, so allow as much time as possible.

American Civil Liberties Union (ACLU)
125 Broad St., 18th Fl., New York, NY 10004-2400
(212) 549-2500
e-mail: aclu@aclu.org • website: www.aclu.org
The ACLU is a national organization that works to defend civil rights as guaranteed in the Constitution. It publishes various materials on civil liberties, including the triannual newsletter *Civil Liberties* and a set of handbooks on individual rights.

Americans United for Separation of Church and State (AUSCS)
518 C St. NE, Washington, DC 20002
(202) 466-3234 • fax: (202) 466-2587
e-mail: americansunited@au.org • website: www.au.org
AUSCS works to protect religious freedom for all Americans. Its principal means of action are litigation, education, and advocacy. It opposes the passing of either federal or state laws that threaten the separation of church and state. Its publications include brochures, pamphlets, and the monthly newsletter *Church and State.*

Center for Democracy and Technology (CDT)
1634 Eye St. NW, Washington, DC 20006
(202) 637-9800 • fax: (202) 637-0968
e-mail: feedback@cdt.org • website: www.cdt.org
CDT's mission is to develop public policy solutions that advance constitutional civil liberties and democratic values in new computer and communications media. Its publications include issue briefs, policy papers, and *CDT Policy Posts*, an online publication that covers issues regarding the civil liberties of people using the information highway.

The Heritage Foundation
214 Massachusetts Ave. NE, Washington, DC 20002-4999
(202) 546-4400 • fax: (202) 544-8328
e-mail: info@heritage.org • website: www.heritage.org
The foundation is a conservative public policy organization dedicated to free-market principles, individual liberty, and limited government. It favors limiting freedom of the press when that freedom threatens national security. Its resident scholars publish position papers on a wide range of issues through publications such as the weekly *Backgrounder* and the quarterly *Policy Review*.

Human Rights Watch
350 Fifth Ave., 34th Fl., New York, NY 10118-3299
(212) 290-4700 • fax: (212) 736-1300
e-mail: hrwnyc@hrw.org • website: www.hrw.org
Human Rights Watch regularly investigates human rights abuses in over seventy countries around the world. It promotes civil liberties and defends freedom of thought, due process, and equal protection of the law. Its goal is to hold governments accountable for human rights violations they may commit against individuals because of their political, ethnic, or religious affiliations. It publishes the *Human Rights Watch Quarterly Newsletter*, the annual *Human Rights Watch World Report*, and a semiannual publications catalog.

Institute for a Drug-Free Workplace
1225 I St. NW, Suite 1000, Washington, DC 20005-3914
(202) 842-7400 • fax: (202) 842-0022
e-mail: nndelogu@littler.com
website: www.drugfreeworkplace.org
The institute is dedicated to preserving the rights of employers and employees who participate in substance abuse prevention programs and to positively influencing the national debate on the issue of drug abuse in the workplace. It publishes the *Guide to Dangerous Drugs*, the pamphlets *What Every Employee Should Know About Drug Abuse: Answers to 20 Good Questions* and *Does Drug Testing Work?* as well as several fact sheets.

National Coalition Against Censorship (NCAC)
275 7th Ave., New York, NY 10001
(212) 807-6222 • fax: (212) 807-6245
e-mail: ncac@ncac.org • website: www.ncac.org

NCAC is an alliance of organizations committed to defending freedom of thought, inquiry, and expression by engaging in public education and advocacy on national and local levels. It publishes periodic reports and the quarterly *Censorship News*.

National Coalition for the Protection of Children & Families (NCPCF)
800 Compton Rd., Suite 9224, Cincinnati, OH 45231-9964
(513) 521-6227 • fax: (513) 521-6337
website: www.nationalcoalition.org
NCPCF is an organization of business, religious, and civic leaders who work to eliminate pornography. Because it believes a link exists between pornography and violence, NCPCF encourages citizens to support the enforcement of obscenity laws and to close down pornography outlets in their neighborhoods. Publications include the booklets *It's Not Your Fault: The One You Love Uses Porn*, *Sex Addiction: Too Much of a Good Thing*, and *Warning: What You Risk by Using Porn*.

People for the American Way Foundation (PFAW)
2000 M St. NW, Suite 400, Washington, DC 20036
(202) 467-4999 • fax: (202) 293-2672
e-mail: pfaw@pfaw.org • website: www.pfaw.org
PFAW works to increase tolerance and respect for America's diverse cultures, religions, and values. It distributes educational materials, leaflets, and brochures, including the reports *A Right Wing and a Prayer: The Religious Right in Your Public Schools* and *Attacks on the Freedom to Learn*.

Religion and Public Education Resource Center (RPERC)
239 Trinity Hall, Chico, CA 95929-0740
(530) 898-4739
e-mail: bgrelle@csuchico.edu • website: www.csuchico.edu
The center believes religion should be studied in public schools in ways that do not promote the values or beliefs of one religion over another but that expose students to such beliefs. It publishes the triannual magazine *Religion and Public Education* and resource materials for teachers and administrators.

Bibliography of Books

David E. Bernstein — *You Can't Say That.* Washington, DC: Cato Institute, 2003.

Cynthia Brown — *Lost Liberties: Ashcroft and the Assault on Personal Freedom.* New York: New Press, 2003.

Michael Chesbro — *Privacy Handbook: Proven Countermeasures for Combating Threats to Privacy, Security, and Personal Freedom.* Boulder, CO: Paladin, 2002.

David Cole and James X. Dempsey — *Terrorism and the New Constitution: Sacrificing Civil Liberties in the Name of National Security.* Tallahassee, FL: First Amendment Foundation, 2002.

Kenneth R. Craycraft — *American Myth of Religious Freedom.* Dallas: Spence, 2003.

Richard Delgado and Jean Stefancic — *Must We Defend Nazis? Hate Speech, Pornography, and the New First Amendment.* New York: New York University Press, 1996.

Alan Dershowitz — *Shouting Fire: Civil Liberties in a Turbulent Age.* New York: Little, Brown, 2002.

E. J. Dionne and Ming Hsuchen — *Sacred Places, Civil Purposes: Should Government Help Faith-Based Charity?* Washington, DC: Brookings Institution, 2001.

Daniel L. Dreisbach — *Thomas Jefferson and the Wall of Separation Between Church and State.* New York: New York University Press, 2003.

Joseph W. Eaton — *The Privacy Card: A Low Cost Strategy to Combat Terrorism.* Lanham, MD: Rowman & Littlefield, 2003.

Louis Fisher — *Religious Liberty in America: Political Safeguards.* Lawrence: University of Kansas Press, 2002.

David French — *A Season for Justice: Defending the Rights of the Christian Home, Church, and School.* Nashville: Broadman & Holman, 2002.

Simson Garfinkel — *Database Nation: The Death of Privacy in the 21st Century.* Sebastopol, CA: O'Reilly, 2000.

Danny Goldberg, Robert Greenwald, and Victor Goldberg — *It's a Free Country: Personal Freedom in America After September 11.* Brooklyn, NY: Akashic, 2002.

Philip Hamburger — *Separation of Church and State.* Boston: Harvard University Press, 2002.

John B. Harer and Eugenia E. Harrell — *People for and Against Unrestricted Expression.* Westport, CT: Greenwood, 2002.

Thomas R. Hensley	*The Boundaries of Freedom of Expression & Order in American Democracy*. Kent, OH: Kent State University Press, 2001.
Michael S. Hyatt	*Invasion of Privacy: How to Protect Yourself in the Digital Age*. Washington, DC: Regnery, 2001.
Philip Jenkins	*Beyond Tolerance: Child Pornography on the Internet*. New York: New York University Press, 2003.
Wendy Kaminer	*Free for All: Defending Liberty in America Today*. Boston: Beacon, 2002.
Milton Ridvas Konvitz	*Fundamental Liberties of a Free People: Religion, Speech, Press, Assembly*. Somerset, NJ: Transaction, 2003.
Nan Levinson	*Outspoken: Free Speech Stories*. Berkeley: University of California Press, 2003.
David Lyon	*Surveillance as Social Sorting: Privacy, Risk, and Automated Discrimination*. New York: Routledge, 2002.
James Magee	*Freedom of Expression*. Westport, CT: Greenwood, 2002.
David Matas	*Bloody Words: Hate and Free Speech*. Winnipeg, Canada: Blizzard, 2001.
William Lee Miller	*The First Liberty: America's Foundation in Religious Freedom*. Washington, DC: Georgetown University Press, 2003.
J. Judd Owen	*Religion and the Demise of Liberal Rationalism: The Foundational Crisis of the Separation of Church and State*. Chicago: University of Chicago Press, 2001.
Paul A. Passavant	*No Escape: Freedom of Speech and the Paradox of Rights*. New York: New York University Press, 2002.
David A.J. Richards	*Free Speech and the Politics of Identity*. New York: Oxford University Press, 2000.
Wojciech Sadurski	*Freedom of Speech and Its Limits*. New York: Kluwer, 2002.
Steven D. Smith	*Getting Over Equality: A Critical Diagnosis of Religious Freedom in America*. New York: New York University Press, 2001.
Lawrence Soley	*Censorship, Inc.: The Corporate Threat to Free Speech in the United States*. New York: Monthly Review, 2002.

Nadine Strossen	*Defending Pornography: Free Speech, Sex, and the Fight for Women's Rights.* New York: New York University Press, 2000.
Alexander Tsesis	*Destructive Messages: How Hate Speech Paves the Way for Harmful Social Movements.* New York: New York University Press, 2002.
Els van der Plas, Malu Halasa, and Marlous Williamsen	*Creating Spaces of Freedom: Cultural Action in the Face of Censorship.* New York: IB Tauris, 2002.
Michael Welch	*Flag Burning: Moral Panic and the Criminalization of Protest.* New York: Alde de Gruyler, 2000.
Reginald Whitaker	*The End of Privacy: How Total Surveillance Is Becoming a Reality.* New York: Oxford University Press, 2000.
C. Michael Williams and Wei-Bin Zhang	*No Greater Threat: America After September 11 and the Rise of a National Security State.* New York: Algora, 2002.

Index